# Body Building Exercises

for the local church

# Body Building Exercises
## for the local church

Eddie Gibbs

A FALCON BOOK

ISBN 0 85491 578 8
First published 1979
Text © Eddie Gibbs 1979
Biblical quotations are from the *Good News Bible* (GNB) and *The New Testament in Modern English* by J. B. Phillips (JBP), © 1976, 1960, respectively
Illustrations © CPAS 1979

10 9 8 7 6 5 4 3 2 1
85 84 83 82 81 80 79

DESIGNED AND PRODUCED IN THE UNITED KINGDOM

*typeset in Baskerville type, printed offset litho and bound by*
Stanley L. Hunt (Printers) Ltd, Rushden, Northamptonshire

*published by*
Church Pastoral Aid Society
Falcon Court, 32 Fleet Street, London EC4Y 1DB

*distributed overseas by*
Australia: Emu Book Agencies Ltd, 63 Berry Street, Granville, NSW 2142
Canada: InterVarsity Christian Fellowship of Canada, 1875 Leslie Street, Unit 10, Don Mills, Ontario M3B 2M5
New Zealand: Scripture Union Wholesale, PO Box 760, Wellington
South Africa: SUBASA, 83 Camp Ground Road, Rondebosch 7700, Cape Town

# CONTENTS

## Text

|   | Putting church growth on the agenda | 13 |    |
|---|-------------------------------------|----|----|
| 1 | Starting from where we are at       | 20 | 81 |
| 2 | Symptoms of sickness                | 38 | 83 |
| 3 | Signs of health                     | 48 | 84 |
| 4 | Using what we've got                | 61 | 85 |
| 5 | Planning for growth                 | 72 | 86 |
|   | Tables                              | 88 |    |

# CONTENTS

# Figures

1    **Suggested course structure**    16

2    **The man–monument axis**    24

3    **Link between electoral roll and communicants**
(*inner-city church*)    28

4    **Variation of average Sunday attendance**
(*inner-city church*)    29

5    **Variation of average Sunday attendance**
(*suburban church*)    30

6    **Sex distribution of Sunday congregation**
(*inner-city church*)    32

7    **Age/sex distribution of Sunday congregation**
(*inner-city church*)    33

8    **Social distributions of Sunday congregation**
(*hypothetical church*)    34

9    **Age/sex distribution of surrounding community**
(*inner-city church*)    36

10    **Congregational involvement**
(*certain church and year*)    64

11    **Congregational involvement**
(*same church a year later*)    65

**CONTENTS**

# Tables

| | | |
|---|---|---|
| 1 | Factors that retard church growth | 88 |
| 2 | Factors that promote church growth | 88 |
| 3 | Planned evangelism | 89 |
| 4 | Community involvement | 89 |
| 5 | Self-evaluation of talents, gifts and ministries | 90 |
| 6A | Spiritual gifts | 93 |
| 6B | Additional gift(s) | 93 |
| 6C | Leadership gifts | 94 |
| 7 | Specific goals | 94 |

# Putting church growth on the agenda

This century has seen the most amazing church growth around the world. According to the Missions Advanced Research and Communications Centre (a department of World Vision located in Monrovia, California), at a conservative estimate there are 55,000 more Christians each day, and 1,400 new churches are opened every week. These facts will come as a surprise to many people. The prophets of doom predicted that the eclipse of western influence in Africa and Asia would cause a severe setback for Christianity. Events have proved them wrong; quite the opposite has happened. In many former colonies, Christianity has expanded even more rapidly in the years following independence.

Despite the fact that the church has been in the growth business for nearly 2,000 years, it is only in recent times that we have begun to examine in any detail what makes churches grow. The pioneers in this field were Donald McGavran, an American Church of Christ missionary, and J. Waskom Pickett, an Australian Methodist, who began to study the progress of the gospel in India during the 1930s. They were concerned to find the answers to three basic questions:

- *Why do some churches grow while others do not in the same context?*
- *Why does the same church grow at one time and not at another?*
- *Why do some parts of the same church grow while other parts do not?*

It soon became evident that, even in those areas of the world which have a reputation for rapid church expansion, such as Africa and Latin America, the growth patterns were very uneven. There was growth in some parts of a country and not in others. And, even within a growth location, the churches of one denomination remained static while others were forging ahead.

The next significant organizational development occurred in 1960, when McGavran set up the Institute for Church Growth in the United States to compare experience on a global scale, to encourage research projects and to formulate principles. In 1965, the Institute, which began in Eugene, Oregon, was transferred to the Fuller Theological Seminary, Pasadena, California. Missionaries and national church leaders from many parts of the world go there for intensive courses on church growth conducted by C. Peter Wagner and other faculty members. They then return to their own countries to undertake research projects as part of their continuing education. The results of their labours are then put to good use. They provide an invaluable source of information in formulating a more effective evangelistic and church-planting strategy.

Initially, the emphasis was directed towards the growth of the church in Africa, Asia and Latin America. Then, in 1972, the Church Growth Institute began to apply some of the principles to the North American situation. The Fuller library now contains an extensive and ever-expanding range of studies. Already, a number of North American denominations and local churches are reaping the benefit of their new insights. However, in terms of church-growth studies, it is Europe which appears as the neglected continent.

While in the United States the church is just about holding its own (with membership at 70% and weekly church attendance at 41%, according to a 1977 Gallup poll), here in Europe we are experiencing serious decline. As for Britain, according to statistics compiled by Peter Brierley for the Evangelical Alliance, the churches are losing 131,000 members and 400 ministers a year.

The principal cause of decline is the lapse of numbers of nominal Christians, whose loss may be of more statistical than spiritual significance; we cannot say for sure until we know the reasons for their departure. If they were no more than passengers, tagging along for cultural reasons, their departure has not altered significantly the spiritual power balance. If, on the other hand, they consisted of people who were spiritually hungry and drifted off because they became bored and disillusioned, their loss is a tragic indictment on the church. If people come for bread and are offered a stone, we should not be surprised if they drift off in search of other bakeries or decide to produce their own loaves.

Thankfully, the picture is not one of unrelieved gloom. There is a brighter side to the picture. There are indications that the inner core of committed Christians is beginning to grow again. Furthermore, many churches are succeeding in attracting young marrieds and their children to family services. However, these hopeful signs are not, as yet, sufficient to alter the general situation. The tide continues to recede, though a growing number of people are coming to believe that it is about to turn.

This book has been produced as a small contribution to that end. It is intended as a practical handbook on church growth to assist those who are concerned to turn the tide. It is geared to the local church situation and is designed to be studied by individuals who are also members of a group. It is not written to answer questions about church-growth theory but to provide a step-by-step programme to help churches to move into a growth position.

What is presented here is not a detailed blueprint but rather a series of exercises to assist churches to develop their own ground plan, tailor-made for their situation under the guidance of the Holy Spirit. Incorporated in the text are response sections to encourage individual reflection leading to prayer and discussion. At the conclusion of the main text, detailed instructions are given for group activities.

As this material is designed, not simply for discussion, but for action, it is important that the church leaders establish an organizational framework to handle the responses from the participating groups before embarking on the course. Failure to do so may well generate

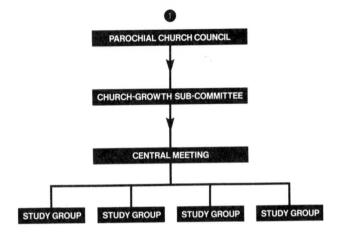

*Figure 1    Suggested course structure for an
Anglican church*

frustration in the groups if they feel that nothing will happen as a result of all the talk. Should this happen, the last state will be worse than the first!

From the beginning, the course must be properly organized. It is no good starting such a venture if you do not have the support of the governing bodies of the church in your area, be it the oversight group of a Brethren assembly or the parochial church council (PCC) of an Anglican church. As well as giving its approval, this group can also supply useful backing to handle the issues which are bound to arise. Its role can be informal or highly structured (see *Figure 1* for a breakdown of a typical Anglican structure).

## Suggested programme

- Hold, in the PCC, a general discussion on church growth, to enlarge the members' vision and raise their expectations.
- Two weeks prior to the PCC meeting at which the course is to be considered, hand copies of this book to PCC members for them to read through.
- At the PCC meeting, secure support for the course. Form a sub-committee (with specific terms of reference) to monitor the reports which come from the study groups and to compile a final report with specific recommendations for the PCC's consideration. This sub-committee should consist of between six and eight persons, its membership not necessarily confined to PCC members. It should be as representative as possible of the various groups which make up the congregation.
- During the months prior to the commencement of the course, teach on themes related to the nature and growth of the church and encourage as many as possible of the congregation to enlist for the course.
- Begin the course by holding a central meeting to explain the nature of the course, to distribute copies of this book and to pray for the Spirit of the Lord to guide his people. Explain that each of the five chapters is to be read and prayed through as a necessary preparation for each of the study-group meetings. Being part of the course commits people to doing their homework.

- Each study group will have a leader appointed by the minister or the church-growth sub-committee and will appoint its own secretary. The course consists of five sessions, which may be held either weekly or fortnightly.
- The summary assessments and recommendations should be handed to a member of the church-growth sub-committee as soon as possible after each session. The church-growth sub-committee may decide to meet on one or more occasions to assess progress during the weeks when the study groups are meeting.
- After the fifth study-group session, the sub-committee should meet: (*a*) to monitor the reports from the study groups; (*b*) to gather additional information on specific details where there has been inaccurate reporting through relevant information not being available to the groups; (*c*) to plan two follow-up central meetings.

Two central meetings will be necessary, covering the same themes as outlined in the course. Their purpose is to draw together the findings from the study groups, to seek to arrive at a common mind and to suggest specific recommendations for the PCC's consideration.

The first meeting should cover:
Starting from where we are at (Chapter 1)
Symptoms of sickness (Chapter 2)
Signs of health (Chapter 3)
The second meeting should cover:
Using what we've got (Chapter 4)
Planning for growth (Chapter 5)
The church-growth sub-committee then draws up its report and presents it to the PCC.

- The PCC considers the report and formulates an overall objective, decides on specific goals and draws up an effective strategy. These are then communicated to the congregation.
- It is then the responsibility of the PCC to initiate action to implement the programme and, at previously agreed intervals, to monitor its progress and evaluate its performance.

It is impossible to design a programme which will exactly fit every situation; so course leaders are advised to read through the book carefully before beginning the course in order to make any necessary adaptations of the material to make it more appropriate for the local church's theological emphases and geographical location.

The subject of church growth, although well-developed in many overseas situations, has only recently begun to be applied in Britain. Many of the ideas are in their infancy. They can mature only as they are tested by experience. The author therefore welcomes any feedback resulting from the reader's practical experience. He would particularly like to know:

● *What aspects did you find particularly helpful?*
● *Which items need altering or refining?*
● *What additional aspects need to be covered?*
● *And, most important, did the lessons learned from this book help your church to grow?*

I would like to thank the following people who have stimulated much of the thinking in these pages: the Rev. C. Peter Wagner of the Fuller Seminary, the Rev. Tom Houston and Miss Janet Harrison, my colleagues at the Bible Society, and the Rev. Gavin Reid of CPAS.

**Eddie Gibbs**

# I

# Starting from where we are at

The most logical place to start anything is at the beginning. However, when we are planning for church growth, we are not starting from scratch. In most cases, we already have a congregation. Our church has probably been there for a number of years, perhaps for centuries. During that time, we have established our image. We have created some kind of impression on the neighbourhood and district. People living around the church have formed their own ideas of what we are like. So we have a reputation either to live up to or to live down!

Before we begin to think about growth, we need to come to terms with three inescapable facts:

- *We are what we have become!*
- *Our situation is very different from that of churches in New Testament times.*
- *It also contrasts with pioneer, overseas missionary situations.*

We are not thinking in terms of churches which are only months old and made up of new Christians. We may worship in a building which has been on the site from Saxon or Norman times. For many people, the thought of worshipping in places with a long, unbroken tradition brings added inspiration. For others, however, such worship is not so much enriched by the past as locked into it.

This danger is not confined to those churches with histories which span the centuries. Most congregations can look back to a 'golden age' in their histories. This may have occurred in the last century or within more recent times. Whenever it was, events in the past have stamped an apparently indelible image on the life of the congregation. Our church may have been established as the result of the growth of population in the neighbourhood, through a spiritual awakening, through ecclesiastical controversy or even through a squabble between families. It may have experienced periods of special blessing through the dynamic leadership of a particular minister or through the vision and commitment of a group of lay people. Many elements from the past have contributed to make us what we are today.

*Reflection*:

> *How would you describe your church?*
> *What are its main characteristics?*
> *What elements in your tradition would you consider to be a help and which are proving to be a hindrance?*

The fact that each church has its own history and character and that every location has its own peculiar characteristics is significant for both renewal and outreach. Often this has been disregarded or underplayed, with the result that many diocesan calls to mission and inter-church evangelistic campaigns failed to mobilize the Christian community. Their efforts may have been well-planned and imaginative, but they did not start where the majority of churches were at, nor did they allow sufficiently for the churches being at different states of readiness. Their beginning was consequently like the start of a shambolic horse race in which the horses, instead of all being lined up in the starting boxes ready to go, were totally disorganized. Some were facing the wrong way, some were refusing their mounts, a few were already cantering up the course, while the majority hadn't even left the paddock!

Sometimes, it is not a central organization but the local church itself which fails to take account of local circumstances. Not infrequently, groups of Christians have become enthused about some recipe for renewal or an evangelistic plan which has worked well elsewhere. They have then tried to import the scheme lock, stock and barrel into their set-up, only to find that they cannot make it work. When they tried to operate that way, it seemed phoney and was clearly ineffective. The lesson to be learned is that the kind of plans which we adopt from elsewhere or develop ourselves must be appropriate to the kind of people that we are and the direction in which God is leading us at that particular time.

## Christians can fade

When local churches begin to talk seriously about renewal and growth, sooner or later it becomes clear that such developments will inevitably mean a shake-up for the members. Many of us have been around for a long time! We may have forgotten the excitement and newness of discovering Christ and being embraced by his love. With the passage of time, our love for him may have cooled off. During our years in the church, we have accumulated a number of jobs, but these are now carried out more from a sense of duty than devotion. We have turned what was intended to be an adventurous pilgrimage into the unknown into the predictable routine of yet another lap of the all-too-familiar track. We have become so programmed that we are almost neurotic at the thought of breaking out of our routine and doing something different for a change. Once we are established in the institution, we tend to be slow to question our traditions and reluctant to ask ourselves about their value for today.

Linked with the tendency to conform is the danger of compromise. We obliterate the situation requiring urgent action by a smokescreen of talk. We dream up every possible excuse to avoid making efforts and taking risks.

> *Once, I set my goal*
> *Further than the eye can see.*
> *Now, I'm nearer to my goal;*
> *I've moved it nearer me.*

*Reflection*:

> *When challenged by a new idea, what do you see first: the possibilities or the problems?*
> *Do you examine the plan to see in what way you could contribute, or do you look for ways of opting out?*

Most human institutions follow a predictable life pattern. They begin with a man of vision, develop into a movement, degenerate into a machine and end up as a monument. There are already a disturbing number of churches which seem to have reached the 'machine' or 'monument' phases. In your church, how aware are you of the living presence of Christ and of his guiding hand? Is there a sense of unity and purpose? Study *Figure 2*.

## People have their prejudices

Most non-churchgoers in Britain have formed some sort of opinion about the church in general and their local churches in particular. A number of varied experiences have contributed to their overall impression: baptism and wedding services they have attended; the church building which they pass on street corners and in the town centre; their churchgoing neighbours; television programmes they have watched. All these elements have made an impression and contributed to their present understanding.

If the church is wanting to relate its message to the people around it, it must seek to understand its market. The leadership must take practical steps to find out what people think about the church and the message it is seeking to proclaim. They must be aware of the inbuilt prejudices and misunderstandings. True communication starts where people are at, not where we want them to be. One way of knowing 'the market' better is through a well-designed questionnaire which can be used on a sample basis among the various kinds of people to be found in the locality. We may want to compare the attitudes of owner–occupiers / council-estate residents; young people / families / the middle aged / the retired; established residents / newcomers, etc. What constitutes significant groupings will vary from place to place. As designing questionnaires and sampling are complex operations, it is advisable to seek professional advice if possible. This will help you to secure reliable data and to know how to interpret your findings.

The data provided by a questionnaire will show what people think of us. We can then ask ourselves if their

## KEY

MAN   There is a vital awareness among the leaders of our church of the living presence of Christ and of his guiding hand.

MOVEMENT   We have a clear sense of purpose but are in danger of relying on human planning and effort; in practice, the Lord is asked to add his blessing to our endeavours rather than consulted in their formulation.

MACHINE   We feel that we are in a rut and that everything has become predictable.

MONUMENT   We realize that, if present trends continue, we shall be struggling for survival, or may even cease to exist, in a few years' time.

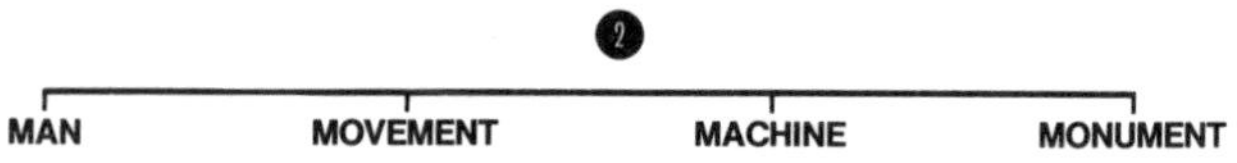

| MAN | MOVEMENT | MACHINE | MONUMENT |

*Figure 2   The man–monument axis; estimate the position of your church*

impression is accurate. If it is, we must then take active steps to do something about it! If, on the other hand, we believe it to be a false image, it is equally important that we devise ways of showing people what we are really like. We cannot change our image overnight. We may have to work hard at it for three to five years before people's ideas begin to change.

The questionnaire might also include a section on personal and community needs. Once these have been clearly identified, the church can then gear its message, resources and publicity to meet people where they are. So much of our programming is shaped to fit our needs and the maintenance of our established organizations and does not relate to the people who pass by. The bulk of our publicity expresses what we want to say in our terms, rather than in the thought forms which enable people to hear. Jesus, the master communicator, demonstrates this principle. When he met the Samaritan woman at the well, he began his conversation with her by talking about water. Addressing the crowds on a hillside he said: 'Look at the birds flying around . . . Look how the wild flowers grow.' (Matthew 6:26a, 28b, GNB.) The secret of communication is to start where people are at. The question is: 'Do we love them enough to exert energy to find out where that is?'

## What kind of people are we?

Sometimes, a major communication problem occurs because the church is not representative of the community and, for this reason, lives an isolated kind of existence. In the case of a downtown church, the neighbourhood may have changed, so that the people who grew up in the church have moved away yet, out of a sense of nostalgia and loyalty, commute back to their church and occupy many of the key jobs. Increasingly, however, they have grown away from the area in their understanding and feelings, and frequently they fail to come to terms with the fact that the locality is no longer the kind of place which they knew in the past. The terraced house, the close-knit community, has been replaced by estranging tower blocks of flats. The white, monocultural, artisan community has been replaced by a colourful, multiracial mosaic.

This problem of estrangement is not confined to the inner-city churches. It can also be encountered in rural congregations. Many villages have been absorbed into the ever-expanding commuter belt of a large city. The character of others has been radically altered by the arrival of retired people who are realizing their lifelong ambition to settle in the country for their sunset years. These migrations can result in the rural church being taken over by the new arrivals.

The presence of an outside voice, or the arrival of 'new blood,' can be a valuable asset. It can lift the horizons of the church beyond the parish boundary. It can challenge irrelevant traditions and rescue the church from complacency. To have other people around, mixing with the locals, can add salt to the soup to bring out the flavour! For, while the church should be deeply rooted in the community, it should not be totally identified. There is always the need for a missionary presence. However, the 'outsider' or 'newcomer' element should generally adopt a low profile. When there is too strong a salt flavour in the soup, it becomes unpalatable.

*Reflection*:

> *What proportion of your church council comes from the locality, and how closely are its members able to relate to the thoughts and feelings of the kinds of people who live in the area served by the church?*

We can learn a surprising amount about our church by drawing together a few significant facts and figures, representing them in graphic and diagrammatic forms, and then trying to interpret, as a group, the evidence that we see portrayed.

## Membership totals

Work out what these have been for the past ten years. You can base your calculations on a number of alternatives. An Anglican church might decide to define membership in terms of electoral-roll totals, or it may have a record of Sunday attendance, which gives a more reliable measure of involvement. In the latter case, arrive at your figure for the year by considering four Sundays in a given month, taking care that it is the same month for each year and that it excludes a major festival, which may introduce a distortion in your figures; then divide the total by four. Alternatively, you may prefer to work from several categories, including (if you are an Anglican church) the electoral roll, the average weekly communicant figure (excluding festivals) and the mean festival communion attendance (Christmas, Easter and Whitsuntide). When you have gathered the figures, plot them on graph paper and join the points together. Look at the graph lines closely. Take special note of any irregularities in the pattern, and ask yourself why the trend altered, either up or down, in a given year. Here are some actual examples.

One inner-city Anglican congregation looked at its electoral-roll totals in comparison with its weekly communicants. *Figure 3* shows clearly that the one-time large pool of people who wanted to be associated with the church (represented by the electoral roll) is rapidly evaporating. This is largely due to the changing nature of the neighbourhood. It is now densely populated with immigrants. It also shows an ageing committed group who are grimly holding on, but each year their numbers dwindle.

The next graph (*Figure 4*) shows the attendance figure of a city-centre Anglican church in the south of England. Spot the year in which the new minister arrived!

The third example (*Figure 5*) is of a thriving suburban Anglican church. This graph shows growth during eight of the last ten years. It raises the question as to why no growth occurred during 1972 and 1974.

When deciding what data to select to portray trends in your church, remember that the objective is not to paint the rosiest picture possible but to give the most accurate indication!

## Age/sex profile

In order to discover this, take an average Sunday congregation and count how many males and females

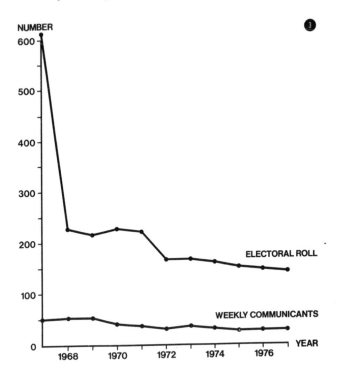

*Figure 3    Ten-year variation of electoral-roll total and
average weekly communicant figure for one inner-city
Anglican church*

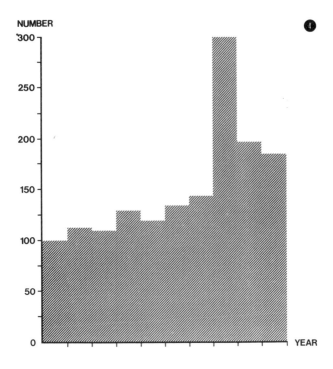

*Figure 4   Ten-year variation of average Sunday attendance for another inner-city Anglican church*

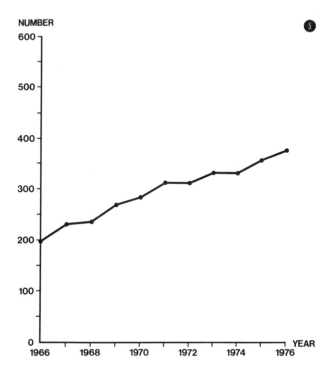

*Figure 5   Ten-year variation of average Sunday
attendance for one (thriving) suburban Anglican church*

are present; then work out the percentages and represent them on a pie chart. *Figure 6* shows one for an inner-city Anglican church.

A further refinement is to represent them according to age as well as sex. In order to do this, you will have to know the congregation well enough to make fairly accurate guesses of their ages! Alternatively, you can ask for this information as part of a congregational questionnaire for the members to fill in anonymously.

When the same church as the one depicted in Figure 6 did this, the results gave the profile we see in *Figure 7*. A large proportion of this small and dwindling congregation is in the upper age bracket and is predominantly female. The older members have seen more change in their lifetime than had occurred during the previous 500 years. On top of this, many of the elderly ladies have lost their life partner. The one thing they don't want to change is their church. This is their one remaining anchor.

### Social mix
What proportion of our members live inside the parish or district, and what percentage come from outside? How many are owner–occupiers, and how many are council tenants? What percentage are unskilled, semi-skilled, blue-collar and white-collar workers? Each of these categories, when represented by pie charts such as those in *Figure 8*, give a graphic indication of the groups which you are attracting.

### How do we compare with the rest of the community?
If we aim to be a church of the community, this should be reflected in the congregational profile matching that of the locality.

### Population figures
Are we located in a declining, static or growing area? If the area is being depopulated, we will have to work even harder simply to stay at our existing level. At the same time, we should seek to develop an effective scheme of

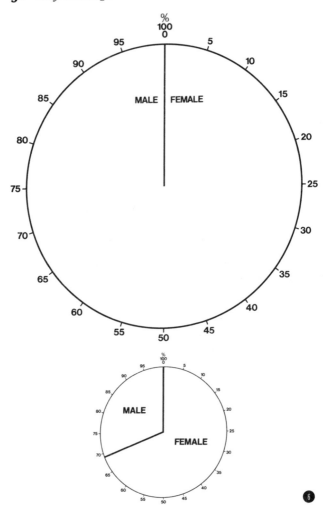

*Figure 6   Sex distribution of typical Sunday congregation in one inner-city Anglican church*

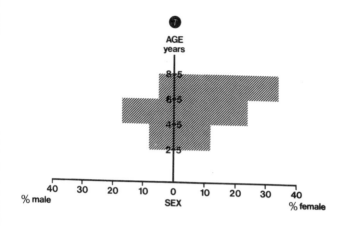

*Figure 7    Age/sex distribution of typical Sunday
congregation in same inner-city Anglican church*

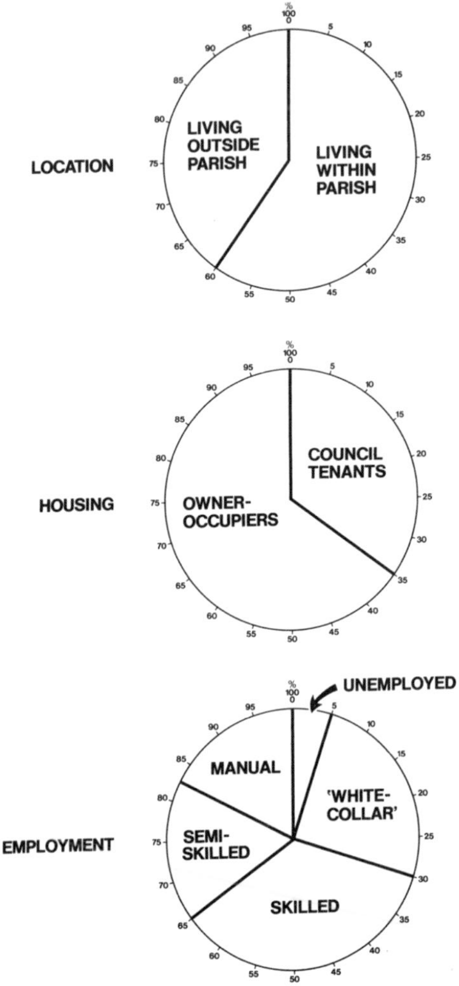

*Figure 8    Social distributions of typical Sunday
congregation in an Anglican church (hypothetical)*

membership transfer. One Manchester vicar had the disheartening experience of every house in his parish being demolished during the first five years of his ministry there. His major task during that period was to link up his congregation to other churches.

If, on the other hand, our community is enlarging, then, all things being equal, we should expect the church to grow and should plan with this in view. Do our attendance figures indicate that we are continuing to attract new people? Where is the new growth coming from? Does it consist of people transferring their membership from elsewhere? If so, our growth represents merely the tidal flow of Christians and not an increase in the size of the total pool.

Growth will probably indicate the need for increased diversity. Is your programme sufficiently varied to appeal to people of different backgrounds and with different needs and tastes? Are we catering for the new people joining us, or are we confining our attention to meeting our own interests?

## Community profiles

Statistics are available from the last census (1971) which give the racial mix, age/sex breakdown, socio-economic groups and housing in your area. It is worthwhile obtaining the data and representing them in diagram form as you did for your congregation. Then compare one with the other. This can be done most effectively by using an overhead projector, laying one acetate sheet over another. Do the two profiles match up? If not, to what extent do they differ? Are you appealing to one age range more than another? Are you catering for the needs of the men as well as of the women?

When the age/sex profile of Figure 7 is compared with that of the community, we can immediately see the difference, shown in *Figure 9*. The church had catered for the needs of the elderly to the neglect of the young marrieds and many single-parent families in the locality. Portraying the situation in this objective manner helped the congregation to discuss the problems they faced in a more open way.

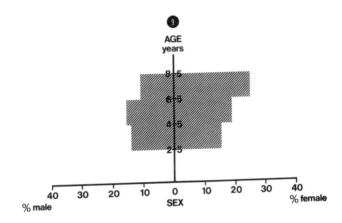

Figure 9    *Age/sex distribution of one inner-city community (same district as for Figure 7)*

The purpose of this chapter is not to urge churches to embark on all of the investigations suggested here. Rather, it is to indicate a range of possibilities for individual churches to select and adapt whichever of the ideas they find to be the most helpful for their situation. We are not interested in statistics for their own sake, only as a means to understand ourselves more fully, to evaluate our performance and to point out those areas where we are particularly weak.

Furthermore, it is recognized that numbers aren't everything, although they do tell us something. The next two chapters of this book concentrate on qualitative growth, which is the other essential aspect. Quantity and quality are equally important. We must not go for one to the exclusion of the other. Authentic church growth means growth in quality and quantity.

## Tailnote
Additional information and advice on congregational and community surveying are available from:

> The Rev. David Wasdell
> Urban Church Project
> St Matthias Vicarage
> Poplar High Street
> London, E1 0AE
> Tel: 01-987 3600

> The Rev. Roy Pointer
> Church Growth Consultant
> Bible House
> 146 Queen Victoria Street
> London, EC4Y 5BX
> Tel: 01-248 4751

**2**

# Symptoms of sickness

The New Testament makes it clear that the church is more than an organization; it is an organism. Paul is fond of describing the church as the 'body of Christ.' The Lord is its head, and we are the organs and limbs, linked through one another to him. It is through his body, the church, that Christ continues his seeking, serving, saving work. He declares to his disciples in the upper room: 'As the Father sent me, so I send you' (John 20:21b, GNB). And to equip his followers for the task, he breathed on them and said: 'Receive the Holy Spirit.' (John 20:22 GNB.) Thus, his body was empowered by his breath. Without this infusion of divine life, the body would have been a dead thing, totally incapable of responding to Christ's commands. But, empowered by his spirit, this originally tiny and insignificant band was equipped to embark on a worldwide mission.

The body of Christ is given a demanding task. 'Go, then, to all peoples everywhere and make them my disciples: baptize them in the name of the Father, the Son, and the Holy Spirit, and teach them to obey everything I have commanded you.' (Matthew 28:19, 20a GNB.) We could not hope to tackle this alone, and it is not the Lord's wish that we should try to do so. He reassures us with the words: 'And I will be with you always, to the end of the age.' (Matthew 28:20b, GNB.) Without the energizing of his spirit, it is futile to embark on his mission. We will lack adequate motivation and resources, and our attempts will prove abortive. So the disciples were commanded to wait in Jerusalem until the power from above came down upon them (Luke 24:29), until they were baptized with the Holy Spirit (Acts 1:5). 'But when the Holy Spirit comes upon you, you will be filled with power, and you will be witnesses for me in Jerusalem, in all Judaea and Samaria, and to the ends of the earth.' (Acts 1:8 GNB.)

We witness as much by what we are as by what we do and say. It stems from a quality of life, that super-abundant life which comes from contact with Jesus.

When someone is about to get involved in an activity which demands great exertion, he would be wise to submit himself first to a medical examination as an essential part of his preparation. Both athletes and astronauts have regular check-ups. Indeed, it can prove hazardous for someone not accustomed to physical exercise to overexert themselves suddenly. Often we don't realise how unfit we have become until we have occasion to run for a bus or gallop up a flight of stairs.

Just as the physical body can become unfit, sick and lethargic, so can the corporate spiritual body. As we have seen, the body of Christ is called to an energetic task, which means that it needs to take very seriously its state of fitness. If the body has become flabby, shows poor appetite, has respiratory problems and lacks energy, it is in no condition to embark on active service.

As part of our preparation, we should be prepared to undergo a medical, to diagnose our ailments and confirm the evidence of vitality. When we know what is wrong with us, we can begin to do something about it. Other-wise, the longer we leave the complaint the worse it may become. Churches, like people, have died because they refused treatment until it was too late. On the positive side, when we are aware of our strengths, we can develop them still further, so that we can do even better.

**Ailments that retard church growth**
Different climates, environments and diets generate different diseases. What is common in one location may be rare in another and totally absent in another. The following church diseases have been identified in this country. Some are widespread; others are found only in isolated cases. As we consider each in turn, please turn to

*Table 1*, where you will find these ailments listed with a space against each one for you to indicate whether you think your church suffers from it (*a*) critically, (*b*) seriously, (*c*) mildly or (*d*) undetectably. Allocate 3 points if you think (*a*), 2 points if (*b*), 1 point if (*c*) and 0 if (*d*).

### 1 Maintenance complex

This is a long-term mental illness which has been with many churches since the First World War. Since that time, the churches have been steadily shrinking in numerical strength and influence in the life of our nation. The one possible exception to this continuing decline was during the Billy Graham visit to Harringay, when some churches, at least in the London area, showed a momentary upturn in their membership. However, tragically, the churches were ill-prepared to sustain the momentum, and an opportunity was lost.

We are not implying that all churches are in a state of decline; clearly, this is not true. Examples could be given of growing churches in many parts of the country, but, as yet, these are not sufficiently numerous to reverse the overall downward trend. The fact that we are emphasizing is that the stance of the majority of churches is maintenance rather than mission. They are preoccupied with the battle for survival, in maintaining what they have. This is reflected in the nature of the agendas of many church councils, which concentrate solely on fabric and finance. For them, any talk of growth is threatening, and they seek theological justification for their smallness and failure to attract new members.

Churches which suffer from the 'maintenance complex' cannot face the demands of raising new spiritual offspring and so preoccupy themselves with the nurture of what they have.

*Reflection*:

> *What resources are we deploying to reach the outsider?*
> *Are church members released for the task?*
> *What training opportunities are provided?*
> *What funds are allocated?*

## 2 Failure syndrome

Whenever a new suggestion is made, the immediate reaction is that it has been tried before; it didn't work then and won't work now. There is a disturbing loss of nerve, which curtails strategic planning and diverts church councils into preoccupation with trivia. On our church councils (or their equivalents in other denominations), we need a new generation of 'possibility thinkers' who really believe that God has a great future for his church and that they are called to be workers together with him.

In many of our churches, there is a lack of the sense of direction. And, when you fail to plan, you plan to fail. We need to pray for a gift of faith to overcome our sense of failure. 'To have faith is to be sure of the things we hope for, to be certain of the things we cannot see. It was by their faith that people of ancient times won God's approval.' (Hebrews 11:1.)

*Reflection:*

> *What is the prevailing atmosphere of my church: is it one of optimism, pessimism or simply apathy?*

## 3 Credibility gap

This represents the chasm between what we claim to believe and the way that we behave. Where the early Christians made an impact, it was because, in addition to declaring the truth that they had found in Christ, they succeeded in demonstrating it. We have to admit that none of us is a perfect representative of the kingdom of God. No-one has achieved perfection, and, the greater the saint, the more keenly he is aware of his shortcomings. Nevertheless, although the church is not to be identified with the kingdom, it should act as a sign and an anticipation of heaven's joys and blessings. It must achieve a degree of credibility in advertising the kingdom. To do this, it must succeed in approximating to its message rather than existing to deny it. The church is called to be a servant of the kingdom of God. As people get interested in the gospel, we should be able to invite them to visit their 'local showroom' with a measure of confidence.

*Reflection*:

> *When strangers come into your fellowship, does what*
> *they experience make them want to come again?*
> *Are you worth knowing as the people of God?*

## 4 Nominality (St John's Syndrome)

It has been called the 'St John's Syndrome' after the first
person to describe the symptoms in the early church.
John, in writing the Revelation, describes the conditions
prevailing in the churches of Asia. With the passage of
time since the founding of these churches, some of the
Christians had cooled off in their love and commitment
and compromised morally to the standards of contempor-
ary society. Revelation was written at a later date than
most of the other books of the New Testament. We
therefore begin to get the problem of second-generation
Christians without a first-generation experience. This
problem becomes widespread and acute where the
church has occupied an influential position in the life of a
nation, so that people drift in in large numbers and on
minimal terms. They then continue their association for
a variety of reasons, partly cultural, partly social. Their
faith is more of an insurance policy than a code of
practice. They choose to believe what they want to,
which may be in direct contradiction to the creed they
profess when they appear at church.

*Reflection*:

> *How much is what I say I believe reflected in the way*
> *that I behave?*
> *Am I a hindrance or a help to someone I know who is*
> *enquiring about the faith?*

## 5 Fellowshipitis

In other words, too much of a good thing! One of the
encouraging signs in the church in recent years has been
an emphasis on the corporate nature of our Christian
discipleship. In our western culture, we have been too
individualistic and fiercely independent. We have flown
in the face of the biblical evidence, which clearly teaches
our mutual dependence. During the seventies, we have
been rediscovering the nature of the church. We are

learning to relate to one another, to share our needs, to enjoy each other's company, to serve our brethren in Christ. Because of inhibitions and shyness, we find it difficult to penetrate beyond the trivial, and in the clumsiness of our attempts some people shy away. Yet, this is slowly bringing a flexibility and freedom that we have not known previously.

However, if this goes on for too long, it can prove counter-productive. We so enjoy each other's company that the appearance of a newcomer in our midst spoils the atmosphere. We can no longer talk about the things that we want to in the way that we have become accustomed to. The cosy atmosphere is suddenly chilled, and we are ill-at-ease, not only with the stranger, but with each other. When this kind of situation prevails, it is a sure sign that 'fellowshipitis' has set in.

*Reflection*:

> *How do you react as a group of Christians when an outreach evening among your neighbours is suggested?*

## 6 Remnantitis

This is 'fellowshipitis in extremis.' Its symptoms are a group of Christians who feel that they are the faithful few living through the days of the final apostasy. Their exclusive preoccupation is their own survival. They are like shipwrecked mariners huddled together in their lifeboat, sending out their distress signals and awaiting the arrival of the rescue helicopter!

*Reflection*:

> *Do you believe that the best years of your church have irretrievably passed, or have you the faith to believe that even greater things could conceivably happen in the future?*

## 7 Ecumania

Some Christians seem to feel that mission must be postponed indefinitely until the divisions within the Christian church have been healed. 'First, we must set our own house in order,' they say. The consequence is that calls to mission are quickly diverted into ecumenical occasions, providing an opportunity to get together and to demonstrate our unity. This is not to say that ecumenism is bad, simply to affirm that ecumenism should not be a replacement for mission.

## 8 People blindness

This ailment occurs frequently in churches located in inner-city areas and on council estates. It is present when the congregation is different socially, culturally and in age/sex mix from the surrounding community. All too frequently, the leadership is in the hands of those who no longer live in the neighbourhood or are from a very different background.

*Reflection*:

> *To what extent is your church representative of the community?*
> *How closely do you resemble your neighbour in dress, type of job, tastes (music, food, etc)?*

Yet, despite the differences between congregation and community, the church makes little or no attempt to bridge the communications gap. It expects people to respond on their terms. To those outside, the church appears remote, and its message is rejected as being irrelevant.

*Reflection*:

> *What sections of the local community are under-represented in the congregation?*
> *If more of these groups came along, would they be likely to repeat their visit?*

## 9 Ethnickitis

In a multiracial area, ethnickitis is evident when, despite the mixed nature of the locality, the church members remain predominantly or exclusively white. The church may feel concerned enough to try to attract West Indians or Asians into their fellowship, but they fail to take into account that every man has the right to find Christ within his own culture. If the church is to fulfil its mission in a multiracial area, it must be prepared to change its patterns of life so that other cultures can find expression in the leadership, worship, fellowship and witness of the church. Unless the church is open to such costly changes, her witness will probably be rejected. The gospel will be ignored or refused, not so much because it is false as because it appears foreign.

*Reflection*:

> *How should the fact that 'we are all one in union with Christ Jesus' be expressed in practical terms in your church? Does it imply that everyone must comply with the dominant group?*
> *How can people from other cultures worship in your church without being forced to change their cultural heritage?*

## 10 Old age

This afflicts decaying inner-city and rural areas, where young people are moving out in search of better housing and jobs and no new people are moving in. The result is an ageing community, which will be unavoidably reflected in the church membership. Unless there is renewal within the locality in terms of fresh jobs and new housing, the affliction will prove terminal.

Having detailed ten diseases of 'failure,' we now conclude with three which are produced by success.

## 11 Overcrowding

This is a rare sociological problem in the churches in Britain! But it does occur in a sufficient number of places to merit a mention. (The author could name several churches which are losing potential members or are beginning to go into decline because they have not dealt with the problem sufficiently promptly!) And, as God blesses our churches with growth, it is likely to become a more common ailment.

This problem begins to appear when our church plant becomes inadequate. The most dangerous moment in a church's life is when the last remaining seat is filled. Our notion of maximum size is often determined by the seating capacity of our building. The size of our plant limits the scope of our vision. As soon as the church becomes full on a regular basis and overfull on festival and other special occasions, frustration sets in. The people who are most conscious of the inconveniences are not the committed 'saints,' who are more highly motivated and make sure they arrive early to park their cars and find a good seat. Those who are most frustrated are the marginal, shall-we/shan't-we? contingent; it is they who turn up too late to park their car and find a seat.

The time to tackle this problem is, not when you are 100% full and in danger of decline, but when you are at 80% capacity and still rising!

*Reflection:*

> *Can you ever envisage a day when you might have to face this problem?*
> *If you already have overcrowding, what's the answer?*

## 12 Structure strain

This further problem of growth relates, not to the physical building, but to the organizational structures.

One could hope that our losses will cover our gains. This is the case with one large Baptist church which rejoices in a capacity crowd. In those years when they have a bumper intake of enthusiastic new members, they have a corresponding fall-out by frustrated Christians deciding to throw in their lot elsewhere. There are only four solutions if you want your congregation to continue growing:

- Enlarge your premises to cope with bigger crowds.
- Divide your church into several congregations, each with its own pastoral oversight and meeting at separate times on Sundays.
- Establish satellite churches.
- Persuade all those who travel long distances to transfer their membership to their local churches; this seldom works.

In some instances, the structure is not only inadequate but also outdated. For instance, at one time, a town in the home counties may have been a popular retirement spot, attracting a large proportion of elderly Christians. Churches mushroom in this 'transit camp for heaven.'

With so many leisured and lonely people around, a full and varied programme develops to service their needs. However, the town subsequently changes its character. It becomes absorbed in the London commuter belt, and the aged saints move on to the 'Costa Geriactrica,' as the coastline between Margate and Bournemouth has been dubbed.

Structures will need to be evaluated and adjusted on a regular basis if the growth is to be maintained. Failure to take prompt and appropriate action will eventually retard growth. When growth is rapid, sustained future planning is essential. We need to ask ourselves: 'If we reach such-and-such a level in five years' time, what should our organizational structure look like?' Usually, this is left until frustrations and organizations call for a period of consolidation. This results in a loss of momentum, which, once lost, is difficult to generate again.

## 13 Leadership tensions

As an organization increases in size and complexity, leadership skills must be developed to cope with the new levels of operation. Objectives must be clearly defined and responsibilities allocated. The symptoms of leadership breakdown are: lack of delegation; vague job descriptions; poor communications, resulting in omissions, duplication and conflict; out-of-touch decision making; and an absence of accountability.

*Reflection*:

> *Are your structures enabling or inhibiting you in defining and accomplishing relevant goals?*

You should by now have completed the diagnostic questionnaire (Table 1), having allocated points as described on page 88. Spaces are provided for any additional ailments of which you are aware but which have not been included in the list.

# 3
# Signs of health

In our previous chapter, we were concerned with diagnoses of church ailments. Now, we direct our attention to the positive side. Here, we are concerned with our actual performance. This section is designed to detect our strengths—to show what we can do well. We undertake this job, not in order to become proud or complacent, but so that we can improve still further on our performance. When writing to the churches, Paul frequently adopted this approach. He commended them for their strong points and then urged them to do even better in future.

Paul writes to the new believers in Thessalonica: 'Finally, our brothers, you learnt from us how you should live in order to please God. This is, of course, how you have been living. And now we beg and urge you in the name of the Lord Jesus to do even more.' (1 Thessalonians 4:1 GNB.)

Car manufacturers are concerned, in their advertising, to emphasize every positive feature of their new models, which are tested out and rated by the motoring correspondents in their write-ups in newspaper and magazine articles. The manufacturers read through these carefully, use any sentences of praise in their further advertising and quietly work to make improvements on those areas which have received criticism. Also, as the new model is tried out on the road, further aspects will come to light, resulting in modifications; occasionally, the model is called in for a defective part to be rectified.

Growing churches around the world tend to display

similar characteristics, despite the fact that their locations are thousands of miles apart and of a totally different nature. Some features will be peculiar to a particular culture or situation, and we must be careful not to make generalisations about these. Once non-transferable features have been excluded, there remains a significant list which is applicable to most situations. The list which follows has been compiled by observing and reading about growing churches, both in other parts of the world and here in Britain. Not all of these features are to be found in every growing church, but there is no growing church which does not display the majority of them.

As you work through the features which characterize growing churches, consider each in relation to your church and see how you rate. *Table 2* provides a form for you to set out your results.

## 1 Positive leadership

This relates, not just to the ordained leadership, but to all of those in positions of leadership within the church. It includes wardens, deacons, PCC members, leaders of organizations and Sunday school teachers. Positive leaders think primarily in terms of possibilities and of making the most of opportunities. They refuse to turn a promised land into a problem land. They do not let circumstances make the agenda but exercise initiative and drive to mould and to change circumstances. Positive leadership refuses to give in in the face of obstacles. It keeps the objective clearly in view and explores every avenue in order to get there.

Here is one minister's vision for his church, located on a housing estate.

ST JOHN'S THREE YEARS FROM NOW

FAMILY

St John's is a family church—a family whose members enjoy serving one another and the community. Its accent is on being the family of God's people in the immediate area—a growing family with hands always stretched out in caring service, to draw others into the family.

The total 'family' is divided up into a good number of 'family units,' each responsible for the care of those who live in its geographical area. These units are made up of the natural families and also the singles, widowed, loners, etc.

Each unit has an appointed leader who is pastor and head of that group. He has gathered about him a small team who share his leadership and discuss, plan and pray together about the life of the group. Many 'family units' subdivided when they grew too large to meet in one home, the 'satellite' groups still being under the direction of that area's overall leader. The leader of each satellite group is also a member of the unit team for that area.

The group meet at regular intervals for fellowship: for Bible study and discussion, relating the word to daily living; for sharing of blessings and problems; for prayer; and for mutual encouragement and support. They are responsible for the pastoral care of their area: e.g. welcoming newcomers, offering help and visiting bereaved and baptism contacts and people in trouble or with marriage problems. They are keen to share the gospel by personal contact and at occasional meetings of the groups, when those with gifts for explaining the gospel speak and testimonies are given. Each group is concerned to help each member know they 'belong' and to discover and use their gifts in the body.

GIFTS

St John's 1981 is especially aware of the need to discover and deploy the gifts God has given to it in every member—by teaching about gifts and encouraging members to recognize and use them in service.

In addition to the house-group family units, to one of which everyone is attached, there are also special service groups for such activities as music, drama and mime, arts and crafts, missionary support, evangelism, pastoral counselling, fabric maintenance, catering, community help, etc.

No-one has more than one main responsibility, though each may contribute to one or two other areas as God leads and time permits.

LEADERSHIP

The leadership of St John's 1981 is in the hands of a team of leaders, of which the curate is simply first among equals. They meet regularly for prayer and sharing of needs, to develop a true fellowship of the Spirit and, from time to time, to check bearings and monitor progress. The leadership team includes each house group ('family unit') leader, service group heads, administrators and those with special teaching ministry, etc, including the young people's work overseer. Members of this team share commonly agreed aims and minister to one another.

WORSHIP

The worship at St John's 1981 is alive! With the aim of giving the best to God, the whole St John's 'family' gather for celebration, teaching, praise, prayer and 'meeting.'

All the gifts which are appropriately used in the worship are regularly employed. (The church building is not a lecture room but a meeting place, to meet the Lord and each other in his family. The furniture and programme are arranged to foster this.) The style of worship varies and bears in mind needs of 'regulars' and 'newcomers.' The teaching is planned to cover broad areas carefully and systematically. The plans are drawn up regularly with much prayer and sensitivity to the work of the Spirit in the church at the moment.

GIVING

The giving is systematic, prayerful and generous. The church moves in the faith that the financial needs will be met as it is obedient to God's will. Many people review their giving regularly, and a good proportion of them tithe.

TRAINING

Training is very important at St John's 1981—for, for example, house-group leaders (in pastoral counselling and care, etc), evangelists (in visiting, sharing the gospel, leading a person to a living relationship with Christ, follow-up, etc, etc), the young people's group, teachers, etc.

BUILDING
St John's 1981 is energetically tackling the problem of a small building. (Alterations for extension could well have already been done.)

THE FUTURE
St John's 1981 is prayerfully considering how to put into effect the plans for which God has given vision for the next three years.

Positive leadership succeeds in inspiring others, so the vision is shared. The test of effective leadership is a simple one: look to see how many are following.

## 2 An agreed agenda

In a growing church, there is a sense of unity and purpose.

The church not only hums with all the activity but also has a sense of destiny. Activity in itself can be a cover-up for lack of objectives. For this reason, it is important to ask, not simply *what* is being done, but *why* and *how effectively* is it being done. There must be an overall sense of purpose. People are working together to achieve a clear goal. Everyone understands what this is, and the congregation are committed to seeing it happen. They are prepared, not simply to giving a nodding assent, but to supplying the resources.

Many churches suffer acutely from the lack of an agreed agenda. It is like the era of the Judges, when everyone did what was right in their own eyes. The minister has his ideas; the curate has different ones; the church council has yet another set of priorities; and the congregation doesn't have any ideas at all, wanting everything to continue as it always has done or to revert to the pattern of some past 'golden age.'

Every church needs to assess to what extent it has succeeded in achieving concensus among its leadership, so that plans receive substantial backing. It also needs to check to see if it is communicating those plans to the general congregation in such a way that they understand what they are all about and are excited about the prospects.

THREE-YEAR GOALS*

- A publication, put through every door three times a year, giving information about the activities of the 'family' of St John's and service offered.
- A 30% increase in average attendance.
- At least fourteen active housegroups within three years (at least seven in one year).
- A 50% increase in giving per member, inflation adjusted.
- Plans for a substantial increase in the church seating capacity over three years.
- A programme of sound teaching in the faith, for all members, led by trained people and using all appropriate resources.
- One church member serving God abroad.
- One candidate accepted for ordained ministry.
- The discovery of at least twelve members with gifts for evangelism plus their training and deployment.
- Recognition and use, within one year, of their spiritual gifts by all active members.
- Employment of a paid part-time church administrator.

*Identified at a meeting of about forty members of St John's during a half-night of prayer, 26 May 1978, after a sharing of basic vision in the leaflet *St John's Three Years From Now.*

## 3 Inspiring worship

In a 'healthy church,' the services are of such a quality that the church members are eager to come. They are reluctant to be absent from a service in case they miss anything. As a result of their coming to the service, they go home refreshed and better able to face the week.

Before the service gets under way, there is a sense of expectancy. From the opening hymn onwards, people want to participate. They are not reluctant to occupy the seats near the front and choose to sit together rather than make for 'unoccupied territory' to stake out! They are not too shy to introduce themselves to people they have not met before or have known only by sight. Friends greet each other naturally.

There is a good rapport between those who are leading the service and the congregation. The choir not only make music but also enhance the worship by giving a positive lead, so that the congregation can follow the melody and are inspired to sing.

A large number of people contribute in a wide variety of ways in each of the services. Apart from singing in the choir, some play instruments in the orchestra; some read lessons; some perform mimes and dances; some bring prayer requests and lead prayers; some conduct interviews and give testimonies; some decorate the church with flowers, banners and other displays; some ensure that the sound amplification and recording is of good quality and that the lighting and heating are right. They all set high standards and show a concern for detail.

The services succeed in attracting and holding a high proportion of the fringers and outsiders who drop in for a variety of reasons. They are eventful in the sense that God is seen to be at work in the midst. Individuals are brought to repentance and faith. The sick are made whole. The congregation sense that they have heard the word of God in such a way that they are challenged to take appropriate action.

### 4 Cultural relevance

One of the basic lessons in communication is the need to start where people are at. The church must find appropriate points of contact by identifying the real felt needs of the people around. It must then speak to their needs in a meaningful way, using understandable language. So often, we speak from the viewpoint of what we want to say rather than from that of what people are ready to hear. Jesus began many of his conversations by pointing to an everyday object or describing a familiar situation.

I asked a leader of a growing house church in east London where he would begin in communicating with his next-door neighbour. 'No problem there,' he replied. 'I would begin with John 15, which speaks of Jesus as the vine and his followers as the branches.' 'Why would you start there?' I asked in surprise. 'Because my next-door neighbour is the only person in the district with a grape-bearing vine!'

Having introduced the gospel in meaningful terms, we must then allow people to apply the message and express themselves in ways which are appropriate to their culture. This has far-reaching application: the emphasis is on our message, our styles of leadership, our decision making, our forms of music and our styles of communication. In a multiracial area, the church must structure itself in such a way that the various groups can participate by expressing themselves according to their culture. In one or two Anglican churches with a sizeable West Indian element in the parish, it has meant the introduction of a steel band alongside the organ and lively, repetitive, rhythmic choruses in addition to the traditional hymns and liturgical forms.

## 5 Multiplication of life cells

Cells are of two kinds: *prison cells*, which confine, and *life cells*, which develop and reproduce. Cell life within the local church should be of the latter variety!

Our church had developed a pattern of house groups. These have helped our members to get to know one another better. There is a growing confidence and mutual trust which is evidenced by people feeling increasingly able to air their misgivings and share their joys and trials. People are now more tolerant of and sensitive to other people, because they are coming to understand them better.

Our leaders are officially appointed and receive training for their job. From time to time, they get together to coordinate planning and to share problems.

A young couple arrived with heavy hearts at their house group on a housing estate in one East Midlands Anglican parish. The other members of the group noticed they were not their usual carefree selves, so asked why they were downcast. They replied that they had been househunting and had just returned from the estate agents after being told that they needed a deposit of £500 to secure their house. They went home that night with £300 and within two days had the remaining £200. This is just one practical expression of the love which characterizes this growing church.

Although our main purpose is to build each other up in the Christian life, we also plan periodic events to attract new members from the congregation to our group and to which we can invite our non-churchgoing neighbours and friends.

There is a strong link between the house groups and the Sunday worship. We are in no sense either a protest group or an alternative to our congregational church life. One feeds into the other. What we learn on Sunday, we try to relate to our personal lives and group discipleship and witness in the week.

## 6 Apprenticeship training

The church programme of activities exists, not simply to serve the members' needs, but also to train the membership to meet each other's varied needs. The training provided covers a wide range of knowledge and skills. New believers are trained in the basics of Christian discipleship and are linked with more mature Christians to help them in their Christian life. Church members are encouraged to participate in evangelism training and visitation programmes to discover whether or not they have a gift in this direction.

The pastors, not only know their sheep by name, but also are sufficiently in touch with them to be aware of their particular talents and gifts. They find out what each person can contribute to various aspects of the church's life and witness. They are alert to the need for these gifts to be utilized and developed. They are seeking out those who, not only do things well themselves, but also are skilled in teaching others.

In the church, people are learning, not simply through listening, but by doing. And, when they are given a job, they are not abandoned to get on with it alone but work under supervision. In this way, the leadership becomes increasingly homegrown. And, if the minister is suddenly removed, it could still carry on without too much difficulty. During the interregnum, things would not simply tick over but could continue to move ahead.

In one Anglican church in the South East, the new vicar was delighted to find on arrival that the church had actually grown faster during the months it was without a vicar. This was a great tribute to the ministry of the previous incumbent who had placed great stress on strong leadership.

## 7 Spontaneous witness

Many people in growing churches feel able to talk about their faith. They know enough about it to speak clearly and convincingly and are quite frequently motivated to do so because they have an on-going personal relationship with Christ. This means that there is always something new and fresh to talk about.

People have made contact with church members or come into the fellowship because they have become curious and fascinated by the way the Christians live or by what is happening in the church. Furthermore, many in the congregation have sufficient confidence in the set-ups to invite their neighbours and friends along without any fear of embarrassment. The church programme is lively and meaningful to them, so they have every reason to believe that it will speak to the needs and hurts of those they invite along—people like themselves.

## 8 Planned evangelism

Evangelism means sharing the good news of Jesus Christ. It means making deliberate attempts to communicate the message of forgiveness and new life through Christ to those outside the fellowship of his church. Growing churches do not allow this to go by default, neither do they relegate it to an occasional activity. It is a regular feature of the church's programme and an essential dimension of many of their activities which are not specifically evangelistic.

A few enterprising churches have recognized that people in their locality are unlikely to be contacted either on the church premises or through homes. As there is little sense of community, with a rapid population turnover, in bedsitterland, they have come up with some novel ideas to contact people. They have posed the question: 'Where do people like to go in our kind of area?' This had led them to open up coffee bars, gift shops and, in several cases, even restaurants, to provide an environment in which people can feel relaxed and in which the gospel can be shared and individuals can be counselled.

The church must bear in mind the various kinds of people in the area and be thinking constantly how its membership can attract the different groups and age ranges in its fellowship. (Complete *Table 3*.)

## 9 Community involvement

We have resisted becoming an isolated ghetto group. We know what is going on in our community, and members of our church are actively involved in many of the neighbourhood concerns—Samaritans, Age Concern, housing associations, day care centres, shelter for battered wives, etc.

Mary was suffering a severe bout of asthma. She couldn't face preparing dinner that morning so went along to the local fish and chip shop on the estate. On arrival, she found the owners, a Cypriot family, distressed and in tears. Mary put aside her own troubles and enquired what was the matter. The Cypriots explained, with animated gestures, that the Turks had moved into their home town, and their relatives had been forced to leave their homes. They were now suffering the winter cold with no more than a tent for protection in a refugee camp. Mary enquired what help they most needed and was told: 'Our relatives and friends need blankets and warm clothing.' She left the shop with the fish and chips in her hand and the owners' burden on her heart. Later, she shared the problem with members of her local church. Within a short while, they had collected enough items to fill two crates to ship to Cyprus. However, the need having been made known, clothing continued to arrive at the homes of church people which had been advertised as collecting points. Soon, neighbours brought, not only their clothing, but also their personal problems, so the collecting points became counselling centres! The community, for its part, feels that it can come to the church for help and backing on specific issues, knowing that it will do its best to give support and exert influence. (Complete *Table 4.*)

## 10 Enabling structures

We have the kind of organizational structure which facilitates prompt and informed decision taking. And, once the decision has been made, we have appropriate back-up to ensure that decisions can be implemented. Our organization is forward-looking, and we budget to allocate funds in accordance with our agreed priorities and with a view to further growth. When there is frustration or breakdown owing to inadequate or in-appropriate structures, we are prepared to look at them critically and to reorganize to meet a changing situation and growing needs.

## 11 Specific, believing prayer

We know what needs to be done, and we believe that, in many cases, God has shown us how to go about it. This means that we can pray in very specific terms and that we are holding ourselves ready to be the answers to many of our prayers. At the same time, we recognize that the task facing us is far beyond our human resources and that we are entirely dependent on the Lord for wisdom in decision making, for the skills and cash to do the job and for perseverance to succeed. Our prayer is therefore all the more urgent. We know that our plans are a venture of faith and that without him our work would not simply become harder—it would prove im-possible. Prayer is consequently regarded as a vital aspect at every stage.

## 12 Life-related Bible exposition

The fact that it has been left until last does not imply that it is of only minor importance. For there to be spiritually significant growth, it is essential for the Bible to be given a central place. Every church service and meeting should be, not only an act of worship, but also a communication event. Preaching is not necessarily the same as communicating. Some preachers fail to realize that, in order to communicate, they must relate what they want to say to what their audience both need and are able to hear. Ministers of growing churches have developed communication skills which enable them so to explain the Word of God that its message is immediately relevant and interesting.

# 4
# Using what we've got

When 'action stations' is sounded on board a naval vessel, every crew member takes up his position. Each is skilled in a particular function and is acting under orders. Some of the crew are responsible for battle tactics, some for navigation and steering, some for performance of the engines, some for the supply of ammunition, some for the accuracy and rate of firing, some for the medical care of casualties, and some for providing regular meals for the entire crew. A naval vessel is not designed to carry passengers.

Similarly, the church is called and equipped to carry out its mission in the world. Christians are described as 'members.' They are members, not of a club, but of a crew. They are not in the church to sit around and be waited upon. They are there to fulfil specific functions. To change the metaphor, when Paul uses the word 'member,' he is speaking of limbs and organs in the body. Each is placed there to do a particular job. A random collection of 'members' does not constitute a body. The right bits have to be there, in the right relationship to each other, linked to the head through the nervous system.

If the local church is to grow, it must ensure that all the members have discovered their function and are kept in good working order. In the human body, when muscles are not used, they become progressively weak. Then, when you suddenly need to use them, the results are painful, if not crippling. If a person is left hanging around, apparently fulfilling no useful function, he will turn into a grumbling appendix.

The New Testament lays down the clear principle that everyone is meant to be doing something to contribute to the life and growth of God's kingdom. How successful are we in turning this principle into practice? Here is one helpful way for a church to assess its progress.

Divide the congregation into four groups, according to their level of involvement. Group A consists of the active, regular attenders; group B of the inactive, regular attenders; group C of the inactive, irregular attenders (these are the 'submarine' Christians who surface at predictable intervals—e.g. carols by candlelight, Remembrance Day, Harvest Festival, Mothering Sunday and perhaps the monthly family service); group D consists of the non-attending members who continue to live in the locality. Estimate how many people belong to each category, then represent them in a bar chart, as in *Figure 10*. A year later, repeat the exercise, as in *Figure 11*. You will then be able to see what progress is being made in helping all members discover their function within the body of Christ.

### Uncovering the hidden talent

In practice, how do we help to discover the gifts that God has given them and to use them effectively? The best starting place is the talents with which we were born and the skills which we have developed in life. The Holy Spirit was active in our creation, and all that we have and are belongs to the Lord. We must therefore encourage each other to ask ourselves what things we are good at and like doing. We need a realistic appraisal of ourselves, avoiding the extremes of arrogance and diffidence.

Paul told the Roman Christians: 'Don't cherish exaggerated ideas of yourself or your importance, but try to have a sane estimate of your capabilities by the light of the faith that God has given to you all. For just as you have many members in one physical body and those members differ in their functions, so we, though many in number, compose one body in Christ and are all members of one another. Through the grace of God we have different gifts. If our gift is preaching, let us preach to the limit of our vision. If it is serving others let us concentrate on our services; if it is teaching let us give all we have to our teaching; and if our gift be the stimulating of the faith of others let us set ourselves to it. Let the man who is called to give, give freely; let the man who wields authority think of his responsibility; and let the man who feels sympathy for his fellows act cheerfully' (Romans 12:3–8 JBP).

There is a right way and a wrong way to go about uncovering the hidden talent in the church. The wrong way is to make out a 'talent sheet' listing all the activities in which the church might like help on either a regular or an occasional basis. Some lists include everything from Sunday school teaching to gardening and duplicating. This kind of approach, which relies upon volunteers coming forward to offer their services, generally elicits few responses and is open to the danger of unsuitable people offering themselves. In many vestries, one finds piles of 'talent sheets' lying around as yet one more good idea which didn't work. Getting it going was like trying to launch a lead balloon.

The right way is to know people well enough to discover what talents and gifts they possess. Members should be invited to contribute on a personal and individual basis rather than through the short-cut, canvassing method of the 'talent sheet.' From the outset, it should be clear from our teaching that to function actively in the body of Christ is not to join a volunteer elite which is prepared to go the extra mile but is a basic requirement of membership. For a church to operate in this way, there must be far more pastoral oversight of the individual member than is generally the case. Pastoring means more than shallow, casual contacts, with personal calls limited to emergency occasions. It implies regular contact and individual attention. We shall look at this more closely towards the conclusion of the present chapter.

The church, then, is intended to be a gift-bearing and gift-evoking community. It has the dual responsibility of helping every individual to discover his gifts and of enabling him to function.

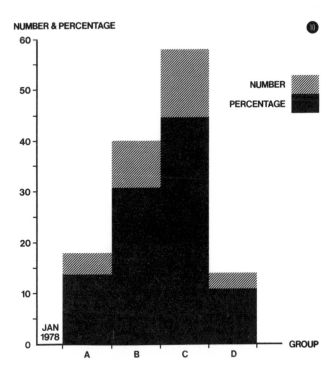

*Figure 10    Degree of congregational involvement
(A most involved, D least involved) in a certain church
and year (hypothetical)*

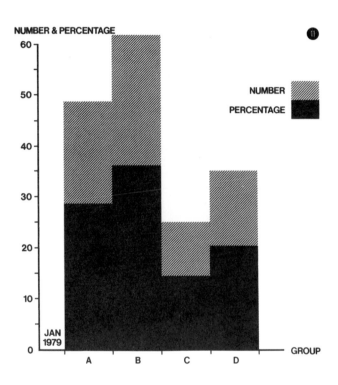

*Figure 11    Degree of congregational involvement
(A most involved, D least involved) in same church
one year later (hypothetical)*

**Talents, gifts and ministries**

There is a great deal of debate among Christians as to how talents, gifts and ministries relate to one another. There are also wide differences of opinion over what constitute spiritual gifts and how some of them are precisely to be defined. Space does not permit us to engage in a detailed discussion of these problems, but a list of helpful books representing different positions and emphases is included at the end of the present chapter. Our concern here is to emphasize that, whatever we understand by spiritual gifts, they cannot be ignored, as they are essential to the maturing and growth of the church. 'It was he (Christ) who "gave gifts to mankind"; he appointed some to be apostles, others to be prophets, others to be evangelists, others to be pastors and teachers. He did this to prepare all God's people for the work of Christian service, in order to build up the body of Christ. . . . So when each separate part works as it should, the whole body grows and builds itself up through love' (Ephesians 4:11, 12, 16b GNB).

At the practical level, it is most helpful to begin with what we would understand as 'natural talents,' because *the natural talent is potentially a spiritual gift.* Among the gifts which are listed in the scriptures is the gift of administration, helps (in classical Greek, this word is used for accountancy), and exhortation and encouragement. In the Old Testament, we read of the Holy Spirit coming upon individuals to equip them 'for every kind of artistic work' (Exodus 31:1–11 GNB) in the construction and equipping of the Tent in the Wilderness. Mention is made there of jewellers, metalworkers, weavers and carpenters. Poetic and musical gifts are likewise special endowments which are used under the influence of the Spirit (1 Samuel 16:18, 19; Mark 12:36). Furthermore, even at the level of national leadership, the Holy Spirit gives legislative wisdom to Solomon and physical strength and military prowess to the Judges.

On the other hand, *the natural talent will not necessarily be converted into a spiritual gift.* In some cases, it is because the new Christian is not encouraged to use his gift for God or may be expressly forbidden to do so. In those churches where guitars and drums are considered to be the devil's instruments and certain styles of music are taboo, the convert will have to renounce his former involvements. In other cases, the talent will not be translated into a spiritual gift, because the person feels that he has misused it so seriously in the past that it has only bad associations in his mind. A further explanation is that the Lord does not motivate the person to use the talent in his service because of the immaturity of the individual. The Lord knows that gift would prove more of a stumbling block than a piece of service. It would lead to pride and self-sufficiency through reliance on the gift rather than on the Holy Spirit's enabling.

We must also recognize that *the gifts given to us by the Holy Spirit do not necessarily relate to our natural talents*. The creative Holy Spirit, not only is active in our birth, but also works in new ways at our new birth and throughout our years of Christian service. Membership in the body of Christ does not simply lead to the redirection and improvement of what we already possess in the service of Christ. We may find that we are given additional, totally new, gifts to enable the church to fulfil its mission. The gifts listed in 1 Corinthians 12:8-10 are chiefly those which are given after conversion. They include faith; the power to heal, to work miracles and to speak God's message (prophecy); and the ability to tell gifts that come from the Spirit (i.e. whether they are really from God, the product of the person's wishful thinking or a satanic counterfeit) and to speak in strange tongues or to explain what is said. It is over these gifts, in particular, that there is so much debate in some sections of the church.

In seeking to discover what talents and gifts we possess, we have so far placed the emphasis on the church's responsibility to draw out our potential for service. Alongside this, the individual needs to examine himself as well. The questionnaire which follows is designed to help those who do not know, or who are unsure, what gifts they have been given. If we are in this position, we should not conclude that we have been left out. 'To each is given a manifestation of the Spirit for the common good.' No-one has been excluded. I've one somewhere, so we had better take steps to find it. Read carefully each of the statements in *Table 5*. Put a tick against those which apply to you, and put a cross against those which don't. Don't be worried at the result. You might end up with far more ticks than crosses, or there might be one solitary tick in a forest of crosses. No-one has all of the gifts, and we may find that we have only one. The Lord deliberately distributes them thinly throughout his church so that we realize our dependence on one another. If you do not understand any statement, place a question mark alongside it, and take your query to the group discussion to see if there is anyone there who can explain it to you.

Two responses are allocated to each gift for two reasons: firstly, in case you cannot identify the gift because of the way the phrase is worded and, secondly, because some of the gifts are understood in different ways according to the theological emphasis in different churches. It is no more than a rough-and-ready guide, but it may serve to clear up a few misunderstandings and help you to identify the possibilities which are worth exploring and developing further. When you have completed the questionnaire, look through it again to see which statements you have ticked. Note the numbers, and draw a ring around those same numbers where they occur in *Table 6A*. (Nos 6, 10, 15, 19, 29, 32, 35 and 39 are covered later.)

The list in Table 6A is a composite one, drawing together many of the gifts which are mentioned in scripture. It is not exhaustive, and there may well be other gifts, which do not appear in the pages of the New Testament, given to the church today to help it to meet the demands of witness in the modern world. If you are aware of having, or if you think you have, a gift of this type, please list it in *Table 6B*.

### Leadership gifts

Although everyone is called to ministry in the sense of serving his fellow believers and witnessing in the world, not everyone is called to leadership. However, as an increasing proportion begins to take an active part, it is clear that effective oversight becomes all the more essential. The New Testament mentions four kinds of leaders. They do not represent a hierarchy of power but areas of specialization required in the New Testament church. They are listed in Ephesians 4:11, 12 as apostles, prophets, evangelists, pastors and teachers. Most New Testament experts link together the last two as generally embodied in one person. These leadership ministries were included in the questionnaire which you have completed. If you ticked any of the questions whose numbers appear in *Table 6C*, draw a ring around the corresponding numbers.

The *apostolic* function represents the church moving out beyond its frontier of influence. The word literally means 'sent one.' In the New Testament, there were two kinds of apostle. There were the *apostles of Christ*, who were eye witnesses of his Resurrection and had lived in company with Christ during his earthly ministry (Acts 1:21, 22); they were twelve in number and have no counterparts today. In addition, there were the *apostles of the church*, who took the gospel into new areas and planted new churches. Sometimes, therefore, the term 'apostle' in this latter sense is translated 'missionary.' However, not every modern missionary is a missionary in this sense. They may be serving the church overseas in a variety of different capacities. They may work within the structures as accountants, secretaries, doctors and nurses, agriculturalists, etc. It is therefore more accurate to confine the use of the term 'apostle' to the pioneer, church-planting kind of missionary. Nor does he have to be working away in some remote, primitive jungle to qualify. The apostle may be found witnessing in the inner city, among an exclusive social set, with particular professions or industrial workers, on the housing estate or deep in rural England!

The *evangelistic* function is the church taking the Good News throughout its network of contacts and range of influence. It operates in, around and through the existing church. The evangelist is the person who can take the gospel where people are. He can explain it in terms which they can understand, and he is used of God to bring individuals to a decisive commitment to follow Christ. The evangelist cannot operate effectively alone. He needs the back-up of local believers who are prepared to support him by active witness. He needs those with the gift of hospitality to open their homes to their neighbours, to provide a congenial atmosphere in which he can communicate. He needs pastors and teachers to build up the new converts in the faith and to integrate them into the local church. It is a rare combination to find a gifted evangelist who is also a good pastor. As one evangelist remarked: 'I like catching fish, but I can't stand having to clean them!'

The *prophetic* function is the ability to declare the word of God and discern the will of God. This function is open to every member as God distributes this gift. However, in one or more, it will be especially evident and more frequently in operation. Thus, he/she will become recognized as a prophet. This role is especially necessary where the scriptures are not available, either because their printing and distribution is forbidden, as in some communist countries, or because they have not yet been translated. Even when the church has the scriptures, it sometimes requires special prophetic gifts to apply the message to the particular situation or to provide guidance on matters which are not covered by scripture.

The *pastoral and teaching* functions are for the care, nurture and instruction of the believers, so that we may understand and apply the truth of God's word. These two roles are closely linked in scripture, because the New Testament emphasis is not simply on knowing the truth but on doing it. The objective is not simply to fill heads with knowledge but to redirect lives through the application of Bible truths. The teacher imparts, and the pastor applies. As there is no distinction between 'pure' and 'applied,' as in maths and the sciences, these two functions cannot be divided and so are normally fulfilled by one and the same person.

There may be other spheres of leadership in addition to these four. In today's church, leadership also needs to be exercised in such areas as music, missionary interest and community service. From your knowledge of the local church and the community in which it is set, think of specific areas in which more effective leadership is needed and add them to Table 6C.

### Booklist on the gifts of the Holy Spirit
*Cinderella's Betrothal Gifts* Michael Griffiths (OMF, 1978)
*Gifts and Graces* Arnold Bittlinger (Hodder, 1967)
*Gifts and Ministries* Arnold Bittlinger (Hodder, 1974)
*One in the Spirit* David Watson (Hodder, 1973)
*Spiritual Gifts and the Church* Donald Bridge & David Phypers (IVP, 1973)

# 5
# Planning for growth

The Gospels provide clear and abundant evidence that our Lord looks for growth of his kingdom. His word is like seed which produces an abundant harvest—30-, 60- and 100-fold. His servants are like farmers, fruit growers, shepherds, fishermen and business managers. They are in the production business. His kingdom is a growing phenomenon. It is like a tiny seed which develops into a sizeable tree. Although the presence of the kingdom stretches beyond the influence of the church, the citizens of the kingdom are the people of God. They consist of those who have responded to the invitation of Jesus, the king of kings. His invitation is issued in the preaching of his word through his heralds of the kingdom.

The presence of the kingdom is intimate. It is both within us and in our midst. It will also become extensive through the worldwide preaching of the message of the kingdom. The growth of the kingdom includes the ideas of both quality and quantity. Both are of vital importance, and one cannot be substituted for the other.

If the Gospels describe that growth is possible, the Acts go on to demonstrate that growth is practical. At the outset, the apostles still had a restricted understanding of the kingdom. They thought it was going to be confined to Israel. The Lord quickly corrected their misapprehension. They were not to sit and wait for the coming of the kingdom but were to be the task force to advance the kingdom. '. . . when the Holy Spirit comes upon you, you will be filled with power, and you will be witnesses for me in Jerusalem, in all Judaea and Samaria, and to the ends of the earth' (Acts 1:8 GNB). This statement was not a pious platitude but a practical programme. The rest of the book of Acts tells the story of how that vision became a reality.

The New Testament shows us that we are in the growth business. But what kind of growth are we to be working for? We need to be clear about this because the scriptures also warn us that not all growth is good. Weeds and thorns threaten significant growth, while foliage is no substitute for fruit. From the outset, we need to be clear as to what we are after. We need precisely defined goals and an effective strategy in order to achieve them.

The church is called upon to fulfil two mandates: to love our neighbour and to make disciples. It is called to a ministry of serving people according to their needs and our resources and to a mission of winning them for Jesus Christ. When these areas are given the priority they deserve, our worship will come alive, because it will be authentic and inspired (see Romans 12:1).

Despite the fact that the scriptures are so clear about what is expected of us, most churches do not work towards objectives. They lose themselves in activities. Their concern is to keep moving rather than to go anywhere. They are like a sailor who has fallen overboard. He is alone in the water and out of sight of land. He doesn't know which way to swim, so he treads water. He knows that the moment he stops he will go down.

Churches are prone to succumb to a roundabout kind of existence. Their life consists of cycles of activities; there are weekly, monthly and annual cycles. However, there is little sense of progress or achievement. Such a concept of time is more pagan than Christian. In the Bible, time is regarded as linear, moving in a line, and eventful, marked by challenge and response. In the Hebrew–Christian tradition, time carries a sense of destiny and, at times, urgency. Time has a qualitative ring about it. Time is a precious commodity; we are held to account for the way in which we use it.

Those 'roundabout churches' need to be sawn off at the base and turned on end so that they become a wheel, capable of going places!

The need to be clear about objectives, so that we know where we are to go, is emphasized in the wording of the Great Commission: 'Go, then, to all peoples everywhere and make them my disciples: baptize them in the name of the Father, the Son, and the Holy Spirit, and teach them to obey everything I have commanded you. And I will be with you always, to the end of the age' (Matthew 28:19, 20 GNB). This command specifies four activities: going, making disciples, baptizing, teaching. Are each of them to be considered equally important, or can we select which we are going to major on? A careful examination of the grammar will solve the problem of priorities.

When we look at the four verbs, we find that there is one imperative and three participles. There is one clear objective expressed by the imperative, that is to 'make . . . disciples.' Making disciples is the name of the game. Discipleship is learning together in the company of Jesus. It is learning, not simply through being given information, but in learning how to use it. Discipleship is an apprenticeship rather than an academic way of learning. It is learning by doing. This is what we are in business for. This is our prime objective.

The other three activities mentioned by Jesus represent our strategy to achieve the goal of making disciples. Firstly, we have to go in order to find, meet and challenge individuals and groups. This encounter will lead to invitation and consequent response. People will want to become followers of Christ. The objective, however, is not simply to register decisions but to make disciples. This means that essential activities must follow the decision, just as the going was essential prior to it. An effective strategy for accomplishing our goal of making disciples must therefore go on to include baptizing and teaching. Baptism signifies initiation. It dramatizes the fact that no-one can simply drift into discipleship. It represents a brand new start and a radically different way of living. It represents death to the old life and emergence into a new one. Thus, the new believer is baptized in the name of the Trinity, for all three persons have contributed to his salvation, and he cannot continue without their presence with him and their power made available to him. The church makes the new believer recognize this dependence on them right from the start.

There is, however, another aspect of baptism which must not be overlooked. In addition to the personal emphasis, there is also a corporate aspect. The new believer, baptized in the name of the Trinity, is baptized into the body (1 Corinthians 12:13). He is thereby introduced into the local church, which has the duty to welcome him in such a way that he feels that he really belongs and where he will begin to function, making his individual contribution in accordance with the gifts that God has given him.

The fourth strategic activity detailed in the Great Commission is teaching. Notice that Jesus emphasized the practical side: '. . . teach them to obey everything I have commanded you.' The goal in our teaching is not simply that men may know but that they might obey. This is in line with what we have already said about making disciples.

If we fail to take action in any of the strategic activities of going, baptizing (initiation, incorporation) and teaching, we will not succeed in our supreme objective of making disciples.

Here, then, is the first basic lesson in planning for growth: *we must have a clear objective and have an effective strategy for achieving it.*

Within many churches, there is, however, a hang-up when it comes to planning. Many Christians feel that we should simply continue to do what we have always done or respond to opportunities as and when they present themselves and leave the results to God. 'We must beware,' they argue, 'of depending on human wisdom.' 'It is not by might, nor by power, but by God's spirit that God's work is done.' Clearly, there is some truth in this position. Human efforts will not, of themselves, achieve spiritual results. On the other hand, nor should we muddle along in a spasmodic way, leaving God to bring order out of the chaos which we have created.

In any work of God, there are divine and human responsibilities. Paul, describing the work which he and Apollos did in Corinth, writes: 'Each one of us does the work which the Lord gave him to do: I sowed the seed, Apollos watered the plant, but it was God who made the plant grow. The one who sows and the one who waters really do not matter. It is God who matters, because he makes the plant grow' (1 Corinthians 3:5b–7). This clearly shows that growth is God's business, but planting, cultivating and harvesting God entrusts to man. Each of these activities requires planning, effort and the application of acquired skills. The ways in which these activities are performed will affect the yield. It is the skilful and industrious farmer who knows how to get the best possible harvest from his soil.

Planning should not be regarded as unspiritual. The gifts of the Spirit include knowledge, wisdom, helps, encouragement and administration. In New Testament Greek the word which we translate by 'administration' literally means the pilot of a ship, and in modern Greek it is also used for an airline pilot. It signifies the ability to steer a right course so that we arrive at our intended destination. This is precisely the skill of management— to devise the route so that we can achieve our desired goal.

*Reflection*:

> *Think back over the past five years. (If you have not been a member of your church for that length of time, consult someone who has.) During that time, have you had a clear objective and a strategy for achieving it? If you did, how widely was it known among the congregation, and to what extent were they committed to accomplishing it? Do you know where you have been going as a church, and in your estimation has it been moving in the right direction?*

The remainder of this chapter consists of an exercise in goal setting in strategy building by outlining eight steps for effective planning. As your study group is not an executive body, your activity will be only an exercise. You are not formulating policy.

**1 Assess where you are and how you arrived there**
This was the purpose of the first of the sessions. Having collected the data, you must now ask what you can learn from your past performance. What things worked out well and are worth retaining? How many of your activities and bright ideas flopped and should be scrapped? Are there any positive clues from the past—things which you could do in a better way and so make more effective next time? On the one hand, there is no sense in repeating the failures, yet, on the other, you don't want to overlook something worth further exploitation.

**2 Define the objective**
This is the most difficult task. From the scriptures, we have seen that there are two stategic priorities: to serve our fellow men and to make disciples. These must then be interpreted to fit the context in which you work. The most helpful question to ask is: 'What kind of a church should we be in order to be effective in service and disciple making?' To determine this requires leadership rather than management skills. The leader should be a man of faith with a vision for the future. Some churches have found it helpful to send their minister away, alone or in company with other leaders in the congregation, to seek God's will for the church and to write down their vision in the form of a brief statement. Until this is done, our activities will be uncoordinated. They will be of the spastic variety. Our church life will remain a frenzy around a void.

For many churches, their goals represent what they happen to be doing. The merit of this way of thinking is that it is fail-safe. It is like firing an arrow at random and then drawing the target around the place where it lands. This ensures that the bull's-eye is hit every time! But it prevents us from asking whether we are doing the right things or from assessing our effectiveness.

However, once we have seen where God has brought us (or our own folly has landed us!) and glimpsed where God is leading us, we can begin to plan our route. We can bring all our resources to bear to achieve our objective.

### 3 Establish goals

This entails focusing on appropriate means to arrive at a desired end. There are many activities which the church could engage in, but, in so doing, it will merely dissipate its energies. Many churches have a long history —plenty of time in which to accumulate a wide range of activities to engage in and good causes to support. Once in a while, it is good to put everything under scrutiny to decide which should be discarded or revamped. Strategic planning means pinpointing the key activities on which you should be concentrating.

An important aspect of strategy building is to establish priorities. Resources are limited, so some items will have to be deleted or postponed. A strategist has the goal constantly in view and refuses to be diverted by the pressures of the moment. There is always the tendency for the immediate to replace the long-term, for the urgent to oust the significant.

### 4 Assess resources

Next, review your strategy in the light of the resources which you consider that you have available. Chapter 4 was designed to give you a more accurate knowledge of the skills and gifts at your disposal. Match the people with the gifts to the jobs to be done. If you find that you do not have appropriate people to fulfil any of your goals, you will need to assess the significance of that item. If you conclude that it is vital, begin to pray that God will supply your need, either by giving it to an existing member or by sending a new person along.

Note that this is not the stage at which to begin costing. If you embark on this too early, your plans are likely to evaporate. Costings should be done on the basis of future growth potential, not on cash in hand or expected income calculated on the basis of the previous year's figures!

### 5 Identify difficulties

This is a planning stage which is frequently mishandled. Some churches are so negative in their thinking that they succeed in turning every promised land into a problem land. In other instances, obstacles are simply ignored. But it is of no use pretending that they are not there, because, when you begin to move, you will inevitably bump into them. Often, careful forethought can prevent the impossible situation from developing when the irresistible force meets the immovable obstacle.

Beforehand, anticipated difficulties should be listed. Some of these may be in the form of circumstances, and others may be represented by personalities. Every potential promised land is littered with walled cities and patrolled by warlike giants.

When movement and change begins to be felt in the local church, there are usually those who, for a variety of reasons, want to pull in the opposite direction. The temptation is then to resist those who are applying the brake by pulling all the harder. This merely results in the opposition redoubling their efforts. Eventually, the tension on both sides will build up until something gives, and the whole enterprise falls apart.

To try to avoid this, it is better to identify the negative influences early on and to attempt to assess their validity. If the leadership knows who the people are who are likely to object, it is a good thing to talk the matter out with them on a personal basis. There may be some valid points made which the advocates of the new schemes have overlooked. Churches are like yachts. A yacht needs a sail to catch the wind, so that the vessel moves along, and a keel to ensure stability. If the yacht were all sail, it would be blown over; if it were all keel, it would go straight to the bottom. Likewise, the church needs both its enthusiasts and its cautious elements.

## 6 Draw up plans

The plans enable you to implement your strategy and so achieve your objective. Care should be taken to avoid their being vague and general. They should be embarrassingly specific, detailing who is to do what by when. In this way, everyone involved will know what everyone else is supposed to be doing at every phase. Unless we are prepared to be specific and build in accountability, it will be impossible to achieve coordination.

### 7 Check progress

It is dangerous to go on assuming everything is going well unless you hear to the contrary! No military commander would operate on that basis; no news may mean that his units have been annihilated! As part of the original plan, there should be specific checks built in at predetermined intervals. By this means, if anything is not going too well, it can be identified early on before it has had time to jeopardize the rest of the operation.

The fact that everyone involved knows at the outset that checks will be made prevents unnecessary embarrassment and offence and additionally acts as a spur to action. When there are no deadlines, most of us are tempted to extend our lines indefinitely.

### 8 Evaluate results

When the plans have been working for a while, look them over carefully. If we find that they are not working, we should be prepared to abandon them. Our plans should be written clearly and precisely—but in pencil and not in permanent letters of gold. There is nothing sacred about them. We must be prepared to delete and rewrite, until we arrive at methods which work. Use *Table 7* for your list.

# Starting from where we are at

1 Discuss the significance of the following Bible verses in relation to church growth: Luke 19:10; 2 Peter 3:9; 1 Timothy 2:1–7; Luke 9:1–5; John 15:8; Acts 1:8.

2 Share where the group members placed their mark on the man–monument axis of Figure 2.

3 Discuss how each group member came to attend your church —e.g.:

- 'Because my parents come.'
- 'Because it was the only church I knew in the area, and I just turned up.'
- 'I was invited by a friend.'
- 'I became involved through one of the organizations or activities.'
- 'I was visited by a church member.'
- 'I knew about the church before coming to live in the area.'

4 How well do you know your church? (Before the meeting, prepare, either on an overhead-projector acetate or on a large piece of card or newsprint, a blank age/sex diagram and three circles: one for the location, one for the housing and one for the work-type percentages. Don't attempt to fill in the details beforehand.) Invite the group to:

- Estimate the age/sex profile of the congregation.
- Estimate the housing mix: owner–occupiers/council tenants.
- Estimate the proportions involved in the following work categories: white-collar, skilled, semi-skilled, manual, unemployed.
- Discuss the significance of the above in relation to the total population mix of the neighbourhood.

5 How has the Sunday church attendance fluctuated over the past ten years? What has been the overall trend: upwards, downwards, decisive change in direction or erratic?

**6** Discuss whether your church should consider undertaking either or both of the following:

- A community survey.
- A congregational analysis.

Submit your conclusion to the church-growth sub-committee.

**7** Pray over the matters which you have discussed.

# Symptoms of sickness

1 What was wrong with each of the seven churches in Asia as reported in Revelation 2–3:22, which describes seven different churches. In what ways were five of them criticized?

2 Before the group meeting, write the list of church-growth ailments on a large board.

3 Work slowly through the list, describing each in terms which best enable you to relate them to your local church situation. After you have dealt with each one, ask the group how many points they have awarded their church in Table 1. Calculate the cumulative total, and write the figure on the board by the side of each ailment. Do this for all thirteen listed. Finally, ask the group if they have identified any others not included in the list.

4 Indicate the 3–5 ailments with the highest number of points allocated by the group. These reveal the areas where the group feels that the church is failing most. Discuss each of them in turn to decide what should be done to treat the condition and prevent its recurrence. (Warning: Some of the above diseases might prove terminal if not detected and treated in time.)

5 Send your list of the most serious ailments and suggested method of treatment to the church-growth sub-committee.

6 Conclude with a time of prayer, confessing failures and asking for guidance as to how to deal with the situation.

# Signs of health

1 The infant church experienced a sudden influx of new believers followed by a steady trickle. From Acts 2:38–47, what activities characterized the early church which enabled it to cope with growth and to sustain it?

2 Ask each member in turn to read out the 'healthy signs' which they gave a good or very good rating for their church. Invite them to give their evidence on which the assessment was based.

3 Are there any additional 'healthy signs' not listed in the growth factors which are present in your church?

4 When all have contributed, discuss whether you think that the combined result represents a frank and realistic assessment. Now compare your 'healthy signs' with the 'ailments' which you identified at the previous meeting. Do the two lists dovetail, or do they contradict each other?

5 Discuss how you might improve on your present good performances in each of the areas which you have identified.

6 Pass on your list with your recommendations for further improvement to the church-growth sub-committee.

7 Divide into buzz groups, three people to each group. Imagine you are drawing up an advertisement to publicize your church in the local press. What would you make the main 'selling points'? How would you show your relevance to meet the felt needs of the community?

8 End with a time of praise, giving thanks for all that the Lord has done through us or in spite of us!

# Using what we've got

1 Ask the group members to identify which of the statements in
   Table 5 they did not understand. Discuss them among your-
   selves until you have arrived at a clearer understanding of the
   meaning and significance of those gifts for the life of the
   church.

2 Turn to Ephesians 14:7–15. Read through the passage carefully, then consider the following questions:

   ● What are the five leadership functions listed?

     Describe each in your own terms. Next, take each in turn
     and relate them to the talents and gifts mentioned in the
     chapter, i.e.:

   ● In what practical ways can these gifts enable our church
     to fulfil its apostolic, prophetic, evangelistic and pastoral
     and teaching roles?

     Be as specific as you can, relating everything to your local
     situation.

3 Draw up a composite list of all the talents, gifts and ministries
   to be found among your group. Discuss to what extent they
   are being utilized in the worship, fellowship, service and
   witness of your church.

4 Do you lack any gifts which you consider to be essential for
   the effective functioning of your church? If so, what should
   you do about the situation?

5 Record your list of gifts and add comments on how they
   could be used to enrich the life of your church and extend
   your ministry in the community.

6 Conclude with a time of prayer, thanking God for the gifts
   he has given and asking for discernment and vision so that
   they might mature through effective use.

# Planning for growth

1 Read Genesis 41:25–49. What do these verses teach about management and planning?

2 Before the meeting, the group leader should draw up the overall objective of the church, as he sees it, according to the second in the eight steps for effective planning and submit it to the group for corrections and additions. Write the final version in the space provided below.

........................................................................................................................................

........................................................................................................................................

........................................................................................................................................

........................................................................................................................................

3 Divide into buzz groups to identify specific goals to be achieved within the next three years in order to realize your main objective. Make a composite list and then go through each item, deciding which you want to alter, delete and keep. Remember a good goal is strategic, measurable, achievable and backed by the group. Do each of these fulfil these criteria? If so, list them below.

........................................................................................................................................

........................................................................................................................................

........................................................................................................................................

........................................................................................................................................

........................................................................................................................................

........................................................................................................................................

........................................................................................................................................

........................................................................................................................................

........................................................................................................................................

4 If the above represents where you want to be in three years' time, how much should you aim for within the first year to be on target?

5 Establish priorities. Place asterisks against three of the goals you have listed to which you would want to give the highest priority.

**6** Allow a few moments for each group member to consider how he could contribute to the achievement of the agreed goals, bearing in mind his/her specific gifts and the time that could be made available.

**7** Identify the difficulties. List below the problems you are likely to encounter when you begin to specify your goals.

.....................................................................................................................................

.....................................................................................................................................

.....................................................................................................................................

.....................................................................................................................................

.....................................................................................................................................

.....................................................................................................................................

If time permits, discuss how you would attempt to deal with each of the difficulties.

**8** Submit your group list of objective goals and difficulties to the church-growth sub-committee.

**9** Conclude with a time of thanksgiving and self-dedication.

# Tables

## Table 1: Factors that retard church growth

| | | Rating* |
|---|---|---|
| 1 | Maintenance complex | ................. |
| 2 | Failure syndrome | ................. |
| 3 | Credibility gap | ................. |
| 4 | Nominality | ................. |
| 5 | Fellowshipitis | ................. |
| 6 | Remnantitis | ................. |
| 7 | Ecumania | ................. |
| 8 | People blindness | ................. |
| 9 | Ethnickitis | ................. |
| 10 | Old age | ................. |
| 11 | Overcrowding | ................. |
| 12 | Structure strain | ................. |
| 13 | Leadership tensions | ................. |
| 14 | ......................................................... | ................. |
| 15 | ......................................................... | ................. |
| 16 | ......................................................... | ................. |

\* 3 points if critical sufferer
2 points if serious sufferer
1 point if mild sufferer
0 point if symptoms undetectable

## Table 2: Factors that promote church growth

| | | Rating* |
|---|---|---|
| 1 | Positive leadership | ................. |
| 2 | An agreed agenda | ................. |
| 3 | Inspiring worship | ................. |
| 4 | Cultural relevance | ................. |
| 5 | Multiplication of life cells | ................. |
| 6 | Apprenticeship training | ................. |
| 7 | Spontaneous witness | ................. |
| 8 | Planned evangelism | ................. |

|   |   |   |
|---|---|---|
| **9** | Community involvement | ................. |
| **10** | Enabling structures | ................. |
| **11** | Specific, believing prayer | ................. |
| **12** | Life-related Bible exposition | ................. |
| **13** | ................................................ | ................. |
| **14** | ................................................ | ................. |
| **15** | ................................................ | ................. |

\* poor/average/good

### Table 3: Planned evangelism

List the special activities that have been designed to attract the outsider to your church during the past six months.

........................................................................................................................

........................................................................................................................

........................................................................................................................

........................................................................................................................

Which do you consider to have been the most successful and why?

........................................................................................................................

........................................................................................................................

........................................................................................................................

### Table 4: Community involvement

List the specific activities to which you personally or church members known to you are giving support. (You may prefer to serve the community through church-related projects rather than through secular organizations. In this case, list some of your activities that contribute towards meeting the social needs of the community.)

........................................................................................................................

........................................................................................................................

........................................................................................................................

........................................................................................................................

........................................................................................................................

........................................................................................................................

## Table 5: Self-evaluation of talents, gifts and ministries

Evaluation*

1  When there is a practical job to be done—like moving chairs, giving out hymnbooks, cleaning or making tea—I usually find that I get involved and enjoy doing it.    ...............

2  When faced with a difficult situation or decision from time to time, I have suddenly seen my way through or been prompted from within by just the right word of comfort or advice for that occasion.    ...............

3  I find it easy to pick up a new song, to remember it and to sing or play it in such a way that other people enjoy it and want to sing it, too.    ...............

4  I have a desire to pray for the sick. Sometimes, I have wanted to reach out and touch the person as I prayed. Afterwards, a number of people have made a remarkable recovery, often beyond reasonable medical expectation.    ...............

5  I like to work my way logically through a problem or project. I find that I can draw up detailed plans to achieve the objective in view.    ...............

6  In the course of my daily life, I have had the privilege of explaining the gospel to people and experienced the joy of seeing one or more put their trust in Christ.    ...............

7  Although the facts were not available to me, I have been able to speak with accurate intuitive knowledge of a situation. Frequently, people who knew the inside story have said: 'Who told you?'    ...............

8  When someone speaks (in tongues), interprets or prophesies, I sometimes feel uneasy, sensing that the message given is not inspired by the Spirit.    ...............

9  I do not feel embarrassed in the presence of a distressed person. Rather, I am frequently moved to weep with them and find that people are uplifted by my presence.    ...............

10  God has used me to reach beyond the church's present spheres of influence, to win people for Christ and to bring new Christian groups into being among neglected groups in my own country.    ...............

11  I have believed that it was possible to go ahead and do something, even though the resources of manpower and money were not available, and found that my faith was vindicated by the vision's becoming a reality.    ...............

*See end of table, page 93

**12** I enjoy entertaining guests in our home. Having them is seldom a burden, despite the extra effort required above catering for the needs of my own family. ...............

**13** Sometimes, my prayers have resulted in an incredible occurrence or chain of circumstances. ...............

**14** I have an urge to express myself by writing, drawing, designing, creating or in dance and drama. In one or more of these ways, I find that I can best convey what I want to say. ...............

**15** Sometimes, I sense that, through me, God has spoken a timely word for the local church which has brought encouragement, presented a challenge or pointed the way ahead. This has been confirmed by the church, who discerned it to be a word from the Lord. ...............

**16** When spending times in worship or intercession, I have found my capacity to express thoughts so frustratingly inadequate that I ceased speaking in my mother tongue and began to utter words and sentences in another language, which I have not learned and could not understand. ...............

**17** I feel a particular concern to visit the sick and elderly. ...............

**18** When, in a Christian group, someone has spoken in an unknown language, I understood what was said, even though I did not know the language that the speaker used. ...............

**19** I can explain spiritual truths in a clear, interesting and relevant manner so that people want to come back to hear more. ...............

**20** As time goes on, I find that my lifestyle becomes increasingly simple, and I don't feel any sense of loss through denying myself luxuries. ...............

**21** I count it a privilege to give an increasing proportion of my income to the Lord's work. ...............

**22** When someone has spoken a message which they claimed was the will of the Lord, I have sometimes felt ill-at-ease, sensing that the person speaking was not living under the Lordship of Christ. ...............

**23** I have a practical bent. I am always making, mending or improving things. I demand a high standard of workmanship from myself and expect it in other people. ...............

**24** When I am surrounded by impossible people or situations, I find I can go on believing that God can bring about a revolutionary change. ...............

**25** Sometimes, a particular need moves my heart or a project captures my imagination, and I enthusiastically give large sums of money towards them. Secret giving, on this scale, brings a sense of joy. ...............

**26** I am able to think through some of the great doctrinal themes of the scriptures and to relate the teaching of one passage to others. ...............

**27** From time to time, lyrics and melodies pop into my mind which express spiritual truths in a way that is meaningful to me and that increase my capacity to worship God. Other people also find their message telling and their music uplifting. ...............

**28** Out of a strong sense of vocation, I have pursued a medical vocation (e.g. as doctor, nurse or physiotherapist) and believe that, in following that calling, I am serving God as well as my fellow men. ...............

**29** For some time, I have wanted to take the gospel and establish new churches in areas abroad where there is little or no Christian witness. ...............

**30** I have an unusual capacity to learn a foreign language with speed and to express myself fluently in it. ...............

**31** When people are depressed and are at the point of giving up, I find that I can say the right word in such a way that their attitudes change and they discover fresh strength to go on. ...............

**32** I long to speak to people about Jesus and feel that one of the most wonderful experiences on earth is to be present when individuals surrender their lives to Christ. ...............

**33** When friends and neighbours are faced with a sudden emergency, they feel free to call on me to ask for help, knowing that, if at all possible, I will give a willing hand. ...............

**34** I can quickly spot flaws when plans are put forward and can make suggestions which help things run more smoothly, because people know what is expected of them and how they relate to others working alongside and in other departments of the church. ...............

**35** People seeking spiritual counsel come to me for advice and to ask for prayer. ...............

**36** I am prepared to renounce all my possessions and pool my income in communal living with other Christians. ...............

**37** Although visitors sometimes feel a little reserved and nervous when they come to our home, they thaw out as they are made to feel welcome. ...............

**38** I have the ability to translate foreign languages. I can do this quickly and at the same time change the way of expressing the ideas so that they sound natural and do not lose the force they had in the original. ...............

**39** When preaching or teaching from the scriptures, the passage I have been explaining suddenly seems especially relevant, and its application strikes home with particular force and authority. ...............

**40** God has used me in the ministry of delivering those who have been possessed or oppressed by evil spirits. ...............

**41** God has given me the facility to apply the scriptures in order to solve a knotty problem. ...............

**42** I have a flair for figures and an eye for detail. I enjoy managing money and keeping account and believe that money should be put to work. ...............

\* √ This applies to me
  × This does not apply to me
  ? I do not understand this

## Table 6A: Spiritual gifts

| | | |
|---|---|---|
| Ability to distinguish between spirits | 8 | 22 |
| Acts of mercy | 17 | 33 |
| Administrators | 5 | 34 |
| Contribution | 21 | 25 |
| Craftsmanship | 14 | 23 |
| Exhortation/encouragement | 9 | 31 |
| Faith | 11 | 24 |
| Healings | 4 | 28 |
| Helps | 1 | 42 |
| Hospitality | 12 | 37 |
| Interpretation of tongues | 18 | 38 |
| Knowledge | 7 | 41 |
| Miracles | 13 | 40 |
| Music | 3 | 27 |
| Poverty | 20 | 36 |
| Prophecy | 15 | 39 |
| Tongues | 16 | 30 |
| Wisdom | 2 | 26 |

## Table 6B: Additional gift(s)

....................................................................
....................................................................
....................................................................
....................................................................
....................................................................

**Table 6C: Leadership gifts**

| | | |
|---|---|---|
| Apostleship | 10 | 29 |
| Evangelism | 6 | 32 |
| Pastorship and teaching | 19 | 35 |
| Prophecy (same as above) | 15 | 39 |

.......................................................

.......................................................

.......................................................

**Table 7: Specific goals**

Within the next three years, we shall endeavour to achieve the following:

.................................................................................................................

.................................................................................................................

.................................................................................................................

.................................................................................................................

.................................................................................................................

.................................................................................................................